UDL

FOR LANGUAGE LEARNERS

Caroline Torres | Kavita Rao

CAST Professional Publishing
UNTIL LEARNING HAS NO LIMITS®

Paperback ISBN 978-1-930583-29-0
Ebook ISBN 978-1-930583-23-8

Published by:

CAST Professional Publishing
an imprint of CAST, Inc.
Wakefield, Massachusetts, USA
www.cast.org

For information about special discounts for bulk purchases, please email *publishing@cast.org* or visit *www.castpublishing.org*

Cover and interior design by Happenstance Type-O-Rama

Printed in the United States of America

For my family whose support and patience while I worked on this, and countless other projects, has always been constant and unwavering, and especially for Kai, who first taught me just how important it is to provide multiple means of representation, action & expression, engagement, and most importantly, multiple means of expressing love. Thank you.

—CAROLINE TORRES

For Précille Boisvert and Jim Skouge, whose dedication to supporting language learners is at the heart of this book.

—KAVITA RAO

CONTENTS

1

Variability of Language Learners and the UDL Design Cycle

“On a typical day, I seek to teach and engage the 30 students in my classroom, each with different strengths, interests, abilities, and interests. Several of my students are language learners who come from various cultural and linguistic backgrounds. Some were born here, and others immigrated when they were younger. Some speak their home languages fluently and are literate in their first language, while others are not. I have learned many strategies to support culturally and linguistically diverse learners over the years, and I use these strategies daily. However, I have also learned that there is variability between my students, and they often benefit from different supports depending on their backgrounds, abilities, and experiences. I realize that as I plan lessons and activities, I need to think about how to use the strategies I know in meaningful ways that take into account the variation amongst my students.”

If you are working in a classroom every day, you likely can identify with this teacher. You may already have experience, knowledge, and strategies that you use to support your students or you may just be starting out. Either way, to fully support and engage our language learners, it is important to understand how learner variability plays a part in language learning and to design lessons that build in flexible options and paths for all.

In this book, we illustrate how teachers can use Universal Design for Learning (UDL) to plan instruction for language learners (LLs). The UDL Design Cycle (Rao & Meo, 2016), which we describe below, is a systematic way to take UDL into consideration while planning lessons. UDL provides a menu of options that teachers can choose from and apply to address their teaching goals and their objectives for student learning. By intentionally designing with UDL, teachers can consider how and when to add flexibility to lesson components to ensure that learners are supported, engaged, and on the path to becoming expert learners.

Chapter 2 describes the importance of integrating language development with content in the classroom and ways to do so. Chapters 3–6 present vignettes illustrating how teachers have applied UDL in the classroom to address the variability of their language learners. These classroom vignettes illustrate ways that teachers can use the UDL Design Cycle to develop lessons that are accessible for LLs and that support them to become expert, self-directed learners. In each chapter, we describe the strategies that teachers use to support their LLs and the UDL connections that address variability of LLs. In each vignette, we present a scenario of a teacher using strategies and design processes in a specific grade and content/skill area. However, the strategies and design processes presented are relevant for teachers across the grade levels and content areas. You will be able to use the strategies presented in all four vignettes regardless of the ages or grades of students you teach.

WHY *LANGUAGE LEARNERS*

Why do we use this term *language learner (LL)*? We use it to mean any learner whose primary language is not the language of instruction. In the United States, English learner (EL), English language learner (ELL), and multilingual learner (MLL) are used in K–12 contexts to acknowledge that learners may speak more than one language, and the language of instruction may not be their "second" language. This is in contrast to the term *English as a Second Language (ESL)*, which is primarily used in postsecondary contexts, and as a result, often in the literature.

When talking about learner variability and diversity, it is tempting to view language learners as the same. The label *language learner* automatically brings our focus mainly to the language acquisition needs of our students; however, their language acquisition is also impacted by many other factors. Language learners themselves are a highly diverse group with widely varying needs related to their different characteristics. The great variability in LLs' academic backgrounds factors into their abilities to learn to read, write, and communicate in a new language. For example, educated LLs who come from countries with alphabets similar to English may have an advantage over educated LLs who are learning a new writing and reading system. Some newly arrived learners have had consistent formal schooling prior to emigrating, while others have had interrupted or inconsistent school experiences. Strong literacy skills in a first language facilitates learning additional languages; weak literacy skills in a first language can impede the acquisition of a new one. Although these learners may appear to have spent the same amount of time in the new country, the way they acquire new literacy skills will differ. Not addressing these differences can result in barriers to academic success, which are described in Table 1.1.

Many teachers of LLs will be familiar with various resources and frameworks to support their instruction. Cognitive Academic Language Learning Approach (CALLA) and Sheltered Instruction Observation Protocol (SIOP) are the best-known frameworks that organize strategies to support LLs in mainstream classes. Another common conceptual framework for support is WIDA, which has been adopted by 39 states in the United States and 200 international schools (WIDA, 2014). WIDA (originally World-Class Instructional Design for All but now just known by the acronym) provides definitions for LLs' stages of language acquisition in alignment to their assessments in the four domains of language: reading, writing, listening, and speaking for English and Spanish. It also has sample performance indicators and teaching strategies to guide teachers in understanding their learners' diverse language abilities. In addition, Culturally Responsive Teaching (CRT; Ladson-Billings, 1995) is getting increased attention for connecting LLs' culture, prior knowledge, and participation styles to make instruction in a new context more relevant and accessible.

TABLE 1.1 Variability of Language Learners

SOME VARIABILITY OF LANGUAGE LEARNERS	POTENTIAL CHARACTERISTICS
Students with limited or interrupted formal education	• Limited or no literacy in the first language, which often causes delays or additional challenges to learning an additional language • Lack of understanding of academic and classroom expectations • Cultural differences in amount and expectations of compulsory schooling • Anxiety or trauma due to documentation and/or refugee status for learners and their families • Difficulty with expectations for attendance • Focus on issues of immediate relevance (academic tasks are typically for future relevance) • Lack of familiarity and comfort with individualistic tasks (particularly individual testing)
New arrivals with prior school experiences	• Limited oral and listening proficiency, but well-developed first language literacy, which supports additional language learning. • Formal schooling in the host country's language resulting in basic understanding of grammar and rules, but difficulty communicating (listening and speaking) • May appear less proficient than they are due to limited verbal and conversational skills • Well-developed study skills and academic expectations, but these may differ in the new education system • Anxiety or discomfort related to shift in identity from a "good" student to a "struggling" student • May have already learned the content but are lacking the language skills

SOME VARIABILITY OF LANGUAGE LEARNERS	POTENTIAL CHARACTERISTICS
Long-term language learner (LTLL)	• May appear fluent in conversation, but have difficulty with academic language and accuracy • Aural learning with limited writing instruction results in "ear learners" who have difficulty making connections between spoken and written forms and who have typically acquired inaccurate, random grammar patterns in their speech and writing • Fossilized errors—incorrect patterns, forms, vocabulary, or pronunciation that they have used for years that they do not recognize as errors and have a very difficult time unlearning. • Frustration and fatigue with being labeled as a language learner for a long period of time • Limited or lacking first language proficiency due to immigrating early or in the middle of schooling in their first language

The clear connection between culture and cognition causes learners to be more likely to succeed when educators build upon their individual cultural and linguistic knowledge and skills (Gay, 2010). This is, in fact, what mainstream students experience, because the dominant cultures are automatically represented in teaching and curriculum. CRT explicitly considers the cultural diversity in our classrooms and "does for Native American, Latino, Asian American, African American, and low-income students what traditional instructional ideologies and actions do for middle-class European Americans. That is, it filters curriculum content and teaching strategies through their cultural frames of reference to make the content more personally meaningful and easier to master" (Gay, 2010, p. 26). In the classroom, this also requires passionate teachers with high expectations for all learners and the belief that they can succeed, which is rooted in respect for all learners and their backgrounds. The deficit model, in which the learner is perceived and treated as lacking, is rejected and instead, the teacher evaluates their curriculum and instruction to make it more accessible and engaging to the learner and follows a learner-centered, learner-driven model.

In this book, we bring insights from language development and CRT frameworks, and blend them with UDL, a set of principles and guidelines for proactively designing instruction to address learner variability (Rose & Meyer, 2002; Meyer, Rose, & Gordon, 2014). In a nutshell, UDL calls for providing all learners with multiple means to 1) access information through a variety of representations, 2) carry out learning tasks and demonstrate what they know, and 3) get engaged and stay motivated to learn. These three UDL principles are further defined by nine guidelines and 31 checkpoints, which provide specific ideas for instructional supports and scaffolds (see *http://udlguidelines.cast.org*).

UDL shows educators how to develop curriculum that reduces and/ or eliminates barriers to learning. By reducing barriers, we can increase access to learning, and support learners in their mastery of skills and knowledge as they become self-directed and expert learners. Teachers can use UDL guidelines while planning lessons, considering where the barriers lie for learners, and then designing activities that reduce these barriers. They can also integrate strategies that engage learners, and design activities that give learners choice and address varied preferences.

Additional Resources

Learn more about UDL by exploring the free online text *Universal Design for Learning: Theory & Practice* at *https:// udltheorypractice.cast.org*. Also, visit the UDL Guidelines at *http://udlguidelines.cast.org*.

THE UDL DESIGN CYCLE

UDL is based on these three essential premises:

1. Learner variability is the norm in the classroom.
2. Variability is systematic and predictable.

3. Barriers to learning can be reduced when curriculum is designed from the outset to account for individual variability.

(Meyer, Rose, & Gordon, 2014).

Knowing that in any given classroom learners will have a range of needs and preferences, teachers can identify some common supports and scaffolds that can be useful for many learners. In addition, teachers can integrate additional supports, as needed, for learners who have specific learning needs. Cultural and linguistic differences can result in varied needs for different students and result in significant barriers to learning, making UDL an ideal framework for supporting language learners.

The UDL Design Cycle (Rao & Meo, 2016) provides a structured way to think about integrating UDL into a lesson plan. Teachers can plan a lesson using the following steps. Figure 1.1 summarizes the steps of the UDL Design Cycle.

Step 1: Identify the Barriers, Preferences, and Needs of Learners.

Teachers should consider what they are planning to teach and consider where the barriers lie for learners. For example, will they have trouble with comprehension? Do they need additional background information to understand a concept? Will learners experience challenges expressing their knowledge in writing? Will learners feel disengaged? How will the variability between different types of learners and their specific needs (e.g., long-term language learners or newcomers) affect their learning and engagement? In addition, teachers can think about learner preferences, needs for support, and specific needs for accommodations and modifications.

This allows the teacher to plan a lesson that integrates supports and scaffolds that specifically aim to reduce barriers and increase engagement. Teachers can refer to the UDL framework as they plan lessons, applying UDL checkpoints to the goals, assessments, methods, and materials of their instructional plan. If a teacher is not aware of the exact characteristics of learners before planning (e.g., before a school year starts), it is possible to consider some of the systematic and predictable barriers, preferences, and needs of learners in general and design with those in mind.

Step 2: Identify Clear Goals.

Goal statements are foundational to lesson planning. Lesson goals are often derived from grade-level standards, and teachers have a particular scope and sequence of the knowledge and skills that learners are expected to gain in a given period of time.

When designing with UDL, it is important to consider what the goals of a lesson are and whether they are stated in ways that allow learners to reach mastery in flexible ways. For example, if a goal statement includes a restrictive verb such as "write," teachers can consider whether it is reasonable to make this more flexible by using a term such as "describe," which allows learners to express what they know in various formats, not just in writing. If the goal has to be "write," a teacher can consider how the methods and materials can include flexible options that provide supports and scaffolds for learners as they work toward the goal of writing. Teachers should write flexible, yet specific, goals (Ralabate & Lord Nelson, 2017).

Step 3: Design Flexible Assessments in Relation to Each Goal.

For each lesson goal, it is important to identify assessments. The assessments allow teachers to evaluate how learners are progressing toward mastery of the goal. Assessments can be formative, summative, or both. *Formative assessments* allow teachers to evaluate learners' progress as they teach a lesson, and give teachers the opportunity to reteach concepts or provide additional help to specific learners who need it. *Summative assessments* allow the teachers to evaluate learner mastery at the end of a lesson or unit.

Both formative and summative assessments can be designed with flexible options, supports, and appropriate scaffolds that take variability into account. A flexible assessment can allow learners to demonstrate their understanding of concepts and their progress towards reaching the goals in varied ways. For a language learner who may not yet be comfortable writing, if an assessment includes an option to communicate orally or allows the learner to work with a partner to plan out a response, the learner will be better able to express what they know and to build confidence in him- or herself as a learner.

Step 4: Develop Flexible and Engaging Methods and Materials.

Methods and materials are at the heart of instruction. By considering how to provide flexible pathways to learning with the use of varied methods and materials, teachers can build in supports that address barriers and provide supports to help students master the learning goals. *Methods* refer to the various strategies a teacher can use during the instructional process, including best practices for language learners. It includes formats of instruction (e.g., presentation, discussion, group work) and tasks or activities that learners will do to acquire content and practice skills. Often teachers use varied strategies already. They can use UDL to ensure that they make intentional choices on how and when to use various strategies to address learner variability. UDL provides a menu of options for teachers to consider as they make decisions about appropriate supports and scaffolds that can be integrated during the learning process.

Materials often go hand-in-hand with methods. *Materials* are the various resources and tools we can use as part of the instructional process to support our methods. These can include anything from paper and worksheets to devices and computers. Providing flexible materials is part of the process of considering the different tools that can be integrated into a lesson to give learners varied modalities and scaffolds during the learning process. The use of flexible materials also entails giving learners the appropriate instruction on using materials (for example, if learners are using a piece of software to do some computer-based activity, teachers should consider whether they need guidance, instruction, or periodic checks as they use the program).

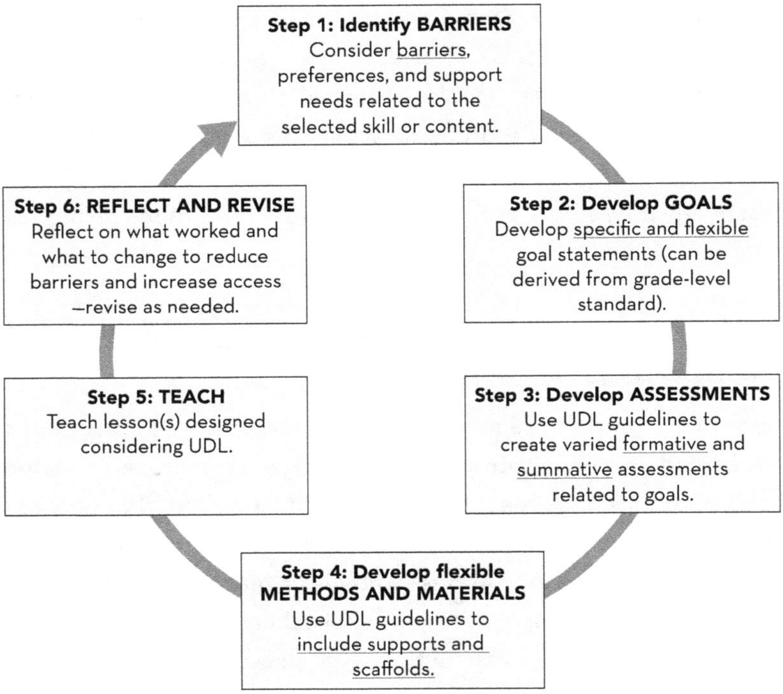

Step 1: Identify BARRIERS
Consider barriers,
preferences, and support
needs related to the
selected skill or content.

Step 2: Develop GOALS
Develop specific and flexible
goal statements (can be
derived from grade-level
standard).

Step 3: Develop ASSESSMENTS
Use UDL guidelines to
create varied formative and
summative assessments
related to goals.

**Step 4: Develop flexible
METHODS AND MATERIALS**
Use UDL guidelines to
include supports and
scaffolds.

Step 5: TEACH
Teach lesson(s) designed
considering UDL.

Step 6: REFLECT AND REVISE
Reflect on what worked and
what to change to reduce
barriers and increase access
—revise as needed.

FIGURE 1.1: The UDL Design Cycle (GRAPHIC ADAPTED FROM RAO & MEO, 2016)

Additional Resources

Ralabate and Nelson (2017) describe how UDL and culturally responsive teaching can be used in concert to design instruction that supports language learners to become expert learners. In their book, *Culturally Responsive Design for English Learners: The UDL Approach*, they provide the foundations for culturally responsive design and describe in detail how it can be applied to dual and second language learners. Their book provides a detailed mapping of culturally responsive teaching strategies and UDL guidelines, presenting a variety of supports and scaffolds that can be used for language learners and highlighting how they can be used to promote a growth mindset, focus on language goals, and ensure that language learners have appropriate assessments and accommodations.

Content and Language Development Integration

2

Language is most effectively and efficiently developed through content-based instruction, instead of through isolated language lessons and classes. When content and language instruction are combined, LLs have opportunities to learn and reinforce language and literacy skills that they need to be successful academically. When language and language development are integrated into content-area lessons and classes, rather than taught as separate language lessons, learners have added context to facilitate their development of language skills. Language learning becomes more purposeful and meaningful, and the new language becomes easier to acquire and retain.

In this chapter, we describe three core areas that teachers can consider when integrating content and language development. This integration supports students in becoming expert learners by fostering a) higher-level thinking and language (grammar and vocabulary) by integrating academic content and discourse and b) student engagement by adding purpose and relevance to their language instruction, since they are being taught content that they need to learn (Lightbown, 2014). Language development requires as many opportunities as possible for the learner to receive input (exposure to spoken and written language), produce output (spoken or written language), participate in interactions, and receive feedback (Crabbe, 2003); simply providing input, even comprehensible input, is only one component of language development support. Thus, teachers can provide the most support embedded throughout their lessons when they provide input, prepare students to respond to the input and produce language, and give feedback (Noji, 2009). This framework can be organized in the following categories of support:

1. Making input comprehensible
2. Providing support for language production and interaction
3. Providing feedback and opportunities to practice

In the classroom vignettes presented in the next four chapters, we illustrate how teachers use strategies in each of these areas as they plan with UDL, and design lessons that integrate content and language development. The vignettes illustrate how teachers can use UDL to address variability and integrate these three core areas of language support, important for LLs, into instruction. The vignettes each have a grade-level example and content-area focus, but they are designed so that teachers of all levels and subjects can identify supports and strategies that can be adapted and implemented in their specific contexts.

1. MAKING INPUT COMPREHENSIBLE

Input must be at a comprehensible level for the learner, yet challenging so that language can be learned and developed (Krashen, 1982). Teachers can support their language learners by making the input comprehensible and accessible—input includes the content and texts, but also teacher instruction, directions, activities, and any other linguistic (language-based) information that the learner needs to access. In order for language to develop, the input must be comprehensible, but the learners also must access and internalize that input and information. Limiting confusion and barriers to understanding through incomprehensible or extra and unnecessary linguistic information, or "reducing the noise" in the language (Noji, Ford, Silva, 2009) in addition to clarifying objectives, making the purpose clear, and building academic background knowledge, are some of the ways to provide this comprehensible input and thus, access for LLs.

a) Identify and State Clear Objectives.

Teachers can start with grade-level standards or lesson objectives and rephrase them into student-friendly content and language objectives. If the goal is clear and comprehensible to the learners, they will be better able to understand what the expectations are for the lesson (Kluger & DeNisi, 1996).

b) Set a Clear Purpose for Each Topic or Activity.

Setting a clear purpose aids in learners' comprehension because comprehension depends on the schema or context and purpose that the learner associates with the topic, and thus, the lens through which they will interpret the information (Prichert & Anderson, 1977). For language learners, having a specific purpose to focus on can also reduce some of the barriers and distractions. For example, if learners are given a narrative text, they can be told to focus on an event that takes place, how the character reacts, and their reflection about the event and their actions after the fact. This allows the LL to focus on only the relevant information without having to understand and process all of the details. To further support this focus on the purpose and help learners organize their ideas, teachers can provide a graphic organizer with spaces for "the event," "reaction," and "reflection."

c) Build Necessary Academic Background Knowledge and Vocabulary.

Having background knowledge in relation to a topic is an essential support for language learners' understanding of input (Echevarria, Vogt, & Short 2004; Marzano, 2004). Learners from different cultural backgrounds or with different academic experiences, particularly interrupted formal schooling, will often lack the *academic* background knowledge necessary to understand the content in school. It is important that teachers assess what background knowledge is required to understand content and support the learners by developing it or making connections to similar concepts in the learners' home culture. Pre-teaching is a common recommendation for working with LLs; however, this is often not effective and teachers should not pre-teach something to build background that the learner can learn from the text.

Teachers should also use visuals and other representations of content to support learners. This can be done by *expanding texts*, which means adding visuals, graphs, and other cues to support comprehension of challenging academic texts (Walqui, 2017). This can also be paired with explicit and focused vocabulary instruction (Marzano, 2004). Making connections to learners' prior knowledge also helps facilitate their understanding and retention of information (Chamot & O'Malley, 1994) and facilitates the comprehensibility of input.

d) Be Mindful of Our Own Discourse.

Teachers should be aware of how and what they say, making their own "teacher talk" as easy to understand and free of linguistic "noise" as possible. This is especially true for assignments and directions given in class. For example, it is useful to provide written step-by-step directions (or directions with graphics) in addition to verbal instructions.

2. PROVIDING SUPPORT FOR LANGUAGE PRODUCTION AND INTERACTION

Learners need support, often called "scaffolding", in order to learn and develop language. Instructional scaffolding can support language learners to produce language at a higher level than what they can do independently (Walqui, 2006). Thus, scaffolding can be provided in the form of a variety of supports that allow learners to access and participate in instruction successfully, and for language learners, to understand and produce language that they would not be able to do without the support. These supports can be curricular, procedural, or facilitated through interaction, and the supports should be gradually reduced as students become proficient at a particular level

(Walqi, 2006). This helps students increase their proficiency and self-confidence.

a) Use Strategies and Scaffolds to Facilitate and Develop Language Production.

One simple support, or scaffold, is to identify the language that learners will need to produce to participate in instruction or to complete an assignment or activity, and teach the necessary vocabulary or grammar structures in that context. Some common forms of instructional scaffolding that help support language production are graphic organizers, which help learners organize and demonstrate relationships between concepts; guided notes, which provide prompts to guide note-taking; and sentence frames and sentence starters, which provide a model of a complete academic sentence, but with one or more words missing that the learner completes with their ideas and vocabulary; and peer support.

b) Provide Sufficient Wait Time and Contextual Support.

Another important, yet often overlooked, support is to provide sufficient wait time for learners to process the input (e.g., a text, teacher's instructions), think of their ideas, and then think of how to express those ideas in the target language. Wait time will vary depending on each learner's individual needs; however, increased wait time typically results in better responses (Tsui, 1996). Individual learners will also have varied challenges producing language due to cultural differences, so if teachers can contextualize the instruction, which means to make real-world connections and provide relevance for learners, they will be better supported to engage in instruction, as well as to produce relevant and meaningful language through personal connections to the content (CREDE, 2004). First language support can also be very helpful for second language development because it allows learners to access their higher-level cognitive functions (Storch & Wigglesworth, 2003).

c) Actively Foster Interactions in the Target Language.

Because language is communication, true language development cannot occur without interaction in the *target language*, or the language being learned. Interaction can occur through instructional conversations and collaborative, group, or pair work. In all interactions, learners have opportunities to receive input by listening to another learner or the teacher, produce output by responding, and receive feedback. Thus, interaction is a very powerful learning tool because it combines all of the components necessary for language development. Cooperative learning also provides language-rich situations through which learners use both academic and social language to negotiate meaning and complete tasks together. Elements that optimize cooperative learning are groups including both native speakers and language learners, as well as learners with different abilities; positive interdependence (all members of the group rely on each other to succeed), individual accountability (members of the group have their own specific task that they are accountable for); intentional development of social skills and related language for negotiating, turn taking, and other functions; and a reflective component of the process (Johnson & Johnson, 1999). Cooperative learning allows language learners in particular to understand and produce language at a higher level than what they can do independently, because the group will always have greater language knowledge than an individual (Dobao, 2012).

d) Be Mindful of Issues Related to Collaborative and Individual Work.

Although collaborative learning can facilitate learning and language learning, culturally the preference and comfort level for working independently, in pairs, or in groups can vary widely. Learners from more collectivist cultures often will perform better and will feel more confident when they are allowed to collaborate with peers. Students will also have personal preferences about whether they like to work collaboratively or independently. Even the gender makeup of groups and pairs can enhance or inhibit learners' comfort level depending on their cultural preferences and experiences (Jordan, 1995).

It can be helpful for teachers to try to determine these preferences and then provide varied opportunities for individual, pair, and group work. For pair and group work, explicit expectations, guidelines, and sentence frames can be provided to help clarify the expectations and allow learners to participate more successfully and more comfortably. Teachers can also group learners to allow for some native language support, which can aid in language development. However, this also needs to be done carefully so that there are not groups where learners who speak a different first language are being left out.

Another factor to consider is that often higher-level learners are placed with lower-level learners to help them, and this can become frustrating to the higher-level learners who may prefer to work independently at a faster rate. In these situations, it can be helpful to group learners strategically, and ensure that the higher-level learner has a meaningful role in the group, so that they don't feel that their learning is being replaced by being a peer tutor. They can also be taught that people learn and retain information better if they can teach it to someone, so they are solidifying their own learning and understanding by helping their peers. This type of awareness and structure is built in to effective collaborative strategies like peer tutoring, Collaborative Strategic Reading, and Reciprocal Teaching (Brown & Palincsar, 1985; Klingner & Vaughn, 1996; Mathes, Howard, Allen, & Fuchs, 1998).

3. PROVIDING FEEDBACK AND OPPORTUNITIES FOR PRACTICE

In order for learners to become proficient in a language, they need extensive opportunities for direct and indirect forms of feedback (Crabbe, 2003). Indirect feedback can be the learner not receiving the response that they expected or having someone demonstrate that they don't understand by asking them to repeat themselves or showing confusion. Direct feedback can come in the form of praise for something done correctly or a correction or *recast*, which is a correct restatement of an incorrect form. Language will not develop if learners do not receive feedback to know what they are doing and understanding correctly and what they are not.

a) Integrate a Cycle of Mastery-oriented Feedback Throughout the Lesson.

Feedback can be viewed and implemented as a three-part cycle consisting of feed-up, feedback, and feed-forward (Fisher & Frey, 2009). *Feed-up* is setting clear expectations and preparing the learner for instruction. This also sets the focus for the strategies and opportunities that teachers choose to check for understanding. *Feedback*, then, is what is traditionally thought of as feedback, but intentionally connected to the feed-up/lesson objective. In addition to traditional feedback given on student work, mastery-oriented feedback can also be "just-in-time" feedback in which the teacher provides support at the moment that the learner needs help or is making an error. Teachers can further give "on demand" feedback when learners ask for assistance; however, this often must be taught because many learners are not comfortable asking questions or for help for cultural or personal reasons.

Often neglected, yet essential, learners also need opportunities to use the feedback to practice the language more in order for it to be developed (Crabbe, 2003)—the instructor cannot stop after the feedback is given and then move on to a new topic. The final, yet essential, component of the cycle is *feed-up*, which is using information gained from checking for understanding and other formative assessments, such as learner work, to identify content or skills that need to be retaught or modeled again because learners didn't understand, or what needs to be reviewed and revisited to ensure retention (Hattie & Timperley, 2007). In addition to this cycle of feedback, learners also need to develop metacognition and awareness of language and the language learning strategies that they are using in order to become more independent learners.

Focusing on flexible supports and modalities through the UDL framework within the instructional areas in which teachers have the most impact; making content comprehensible, preparing for language production and interaction, and feedback and practice will make instruction more efficient and effective for language learners in content classes. Throughout this book, each chapter highlights a content classroom and UDL supports that align with culturally responsive language acquisition strategies to demonstrate how content teachers can successfully integrate language development into their content areas. If teachers keep in mind that it is essential to provide as many opportunities as possible for learners to receive input that is comprehensible, be supported to produce language and interact successfully, and to receive feedback, their learners' language will be meaningfully developed, while their content and academic knowledge are simultaneously developed.

In Chapters 3–6 of this book, we describe how teachers address these three core areas, considering how they can address learner variability. Throughout the chapters, these icons denote how core areas are addressed by the instructional strategies presented:

	Making Input Comprehensible
	Supporting Language Production and Interaction
	Feedback and Practice

3

Developing Reading Across the Curriculum

Chapter at a Glance

Using UDL to address the following barriers and learner preferences and needs:

Accessing Texts and Meeting Reading Standards.

- Foundational reading skills: decoding and fluency
- Context and background
- Vocabulary knowledge

Engagement with Reading

- Attention to instruction
- Sustained attention and reading

Learners' Preferences and Needs

- Varied formats for input (group reading and individual reading time)
- Relevance and learner interest

» Classroom Vignette: Language Arts

Ms. Takayama reflected on some of the challenges she was having in her extremely diverse eighth grade language arts class. In addition to the cultural diversity of her students, her class included newcomers with varied levels of prior formal schooling, and long-term language learners. Due to this variability, she struggled to find reading materials that she could use to engage the whole class; when the level was too low, many of her more proficient students would get bored, and when the level was too high, the newcomers and less proficient students would disengage, resulting in difficulty managing the classroom. It was also often challenging to get all her learners engaged in reading activities in class.

For an upcoming reading lesson, she decided to create a lesson that was designed using UDL and took into account her knowledge of LLs and culturally responsive instruction. Using a text selected by the eighth grade teachers, she planned a lesson that incorporated several supports to provide options for representation, expression, and engagement, hoping to build in various options for reading comprehension that would address the learner variability in her class.

» Classroom Profile

- 8th grade language arts
- 1 general education teacher
- 25 students
- Countries of Birth:
  - 9 China, 14 Pacific Islands (4 Chuuk, 3 Marshall Islands, 1 Samoa, 6 Phillippines), 1 Japan, 1 Vietnam
- Language learner variability:
  - 4 newcomers, 2 with interrupted formal schooling
  - 19 lived in the country 1–3 years, 3 with interrupted formal schooling
  - 2 long-term language learners (LTLLs) 5+ years in the country

THE UDL DESIGN CYCLE: PLANNING A READING LESSON

Ms. Takayama planned a lesson using the UDL Design Cycle (see detailed description in Chapter 1). Knowing the profiles of her varied language learners, she was able to identify barriers and preferences of her students and planned a lesson that integrated supports and scaffolds that specifically aim to reduce barriers and take into account students, preferences and needs. Ms. Takayama uses the UDL framework as she considers the goals, assessments, methods, and materials to use in her lesson. In the following sections, we describe how she undertook the planning process. The UDL-based Lesson Summary (at the end of this chapter) provides an overview of how she applied UDL throughout her planning process.

Step 1: Identify Barriers, Preferences, and Support Needs

Because learner variability is systematic and predictable, Ms. Takayama was able to consider some common barriers and preferences for her students. She started by writing down barriers that many students would potentially face and also noted the specific barriers for individual students, paying explicit attention to barriers to **comprehensible input** in any texts, materials, and her instruction for her varied language learners. She also identified and added some issues related to student preferences and engagement.

Barriers Related to Reading Comprehension

Accessing Texts and Meeting Reading Standards
- **Foundational reading skills: decoding and fluency**
- **Context and background**
- **Vocabulary knowledge**

One major barrier to reading comprehension is **access to the text**. To access text, learners need several prerequisite skills related to reading, such as decoding and fluency. Knowing the context and background of what they are reading and knowing the purpose for reading a text can also increase understanding of relevance for learners (Grabe, 2009). Learners who are unaware of or unfamiliar with the **context of the text** that they are reading or do not have the assumed academic or cultural **background knowledge** (Marzano, 2004), will not be able to access the text sufficiently. Many texts require knowledge of popular culture, academic expectations, and national history, which if LLs do not have, will be difficult to understand. Teachers can support learners' comprehension by making the context explicit and letting the learners know what kind of text it is (e.g., non-fiction, fiction, folk tale, realistic non-fiction) and what the purpose of such a text is. For example, folk tales are often stories that explain something about nature or how the world works. Typically, they also include a message that the reader is supposed to infer about how we should behave in the real world. If learners do not know this context at the outset, their understanding of the text may be limited or changed. In addition, teachers can **build background knowledge** that texts *assume* that the readers have. However, while building background, teachers should be careful not to include information that students should learn from the text.

The **purpose** for reading a text is also integral to readers' comprehension and inferences that they make (Narvaez, Van Den Broek, & Ruiz, 1999; Pichert & Anderson, 1977). If learners are not told what the purpose is for reading, they will set their own purpose, which may not align with the teachers' intended purpose and thus impact understanding. In addition, when LLs have a clear purpose, it can help reduce some of the "linguistic noise" in the text (Noji, Ford, & Silva, 2008) and allow them to focus on the most relevant information to the goal.

Being familiar with key terms in the text is also essential to comprehension. Because vocabulary is highly correlated to academic success and is instrumental in reading comprehension (Marzano, 2004; Nagy & Townsend, 2012), teachers can provide *contextualized* vocabulary instruction to support learners' comprehension (Anthony, 2008). Explicit vocabulary instruction also better prepares learners to respond to the text using the relevant, academic vocabulary.

In a typical classroom with varied language learners, teachers might have 1) newcomers unfamiliar with the orthography of a new language and those who struggle with the basic mechanics of reading, 2) learners who can decode the text, but lack fluency (i.e., speed and fluidity), which interferes with their ability to comprehend the text, and 3) learners who appear to read well but do not understand what they are reading. Once teachers determine the root of why the learner is not able to access a text, they can determine how to apply the appropriate supports as they plan the goals, methods, materials, and assessments for their lessons.

Engagement with Reading

- Attention to instruction
- Sustained attention and reading

To be successful readers, learners need to be able to attend to reading instruction and sustain their attention to passages being read aloud to them, or passages they read independently. Readers who lack fluency can become fatigued by the cognitive demands of reading (Jenkins, Fuchs, Van Den Broek, Espin, & Deno, 2003), and readers who have difficulty comprehending have to expend more attentional resources (Grabe, 2009), which can make it challenging for them to sustain their attention to a text that they don't understand or don't understand well. In addition, different cultural expectations regarding school behavior can result in learners not paying attention the way in which teachers in their host culture expect (Gay, 2010).

In order to support students to comprehend and engage in instruction, it is important for teachers to provide *scaffolding*, which are specific supports designed to help the learner access and perform at a level higher than their current proficiency and skill level (Walqui, 2006). Scaffolding can be viewed at three different levels of instruction:

1. the structured progression of a lesson, the curriculum, projects, and class routines;

2. the specific supports and procedures for a specific activity or part of a lesson, and;

3. structured and guided interaction that facilitates the activity, part of a lesson, or goal (Walqui, 2006).

Learners' Preferences and Needs

- **Varied formats for input (group reading and individual reading time)**
- **Relevance and learner interest**

Teachers should also consider individual preferences and needs in relation to the skill being taught. For example, some learners may enjoy listening to the teacher read aloud, while others may like to read independently. Text-to-speech software, which is now built into laptops and mobile devices, allows learners to see and hear the words at the same time, which can help reinforce the letter-sound correlation, fluency, and recognition of known vocabulary words. Emerging research shows that text-to-speech, hyperlinked definitions, and other computer-assisted reading supports have promise to support reading comprehension for struggling readers (Stetter & Hughes, 2010). When these supports make reading feel easier and more enjoyable, it is easier for students to sustain their interest and focus on reading.

Learners may also be motivated to read if the topics and text are of interest to them. Students' engagement in reading and their reading comprehension are highly correlated (Wigfield, et al., 2008), so teachers should try to vary the format and use relevant and interesting reading materials when possible. To do this, teachers can select a variety of texts with varying formats from which learners can choose.

Step 2: Goals

Because setting clear goals is the first essential step in providing effective **feedback and practice**, Ms. Takayama created explicit goals to drive her instruction and assessment.

Ms. Takayama's grade-level team selected common texts that all eighth graders read in language arts over the course of the school year.

Following the team's scope and sequence, the following week, Ms. Takayama introduced an excerpt of a book about Martin Luther King Jr. Ms. Takayama decided to use Dr. King's story as a way to foster discussion about how individuals reach their goals by persisting despite challenges. She considered these two grade-level standards for reading:

Grade Level Reading Standard: Cite the textual evidence that most strongly supports an analysis of what the text says explicitly, as well as inferences drawn from the text. *(Based on the Common Core State Standard for English Language Arts: Reading RI.8.1)*

Grade Level Reading Standard: Determine a central idea of a text and analyze its development over the course of the text, including its relationship to supporting ideas; provide an objective summary of the text. *(Based on the Common Core State Standard for English Language Arts: Reading RI.8.2)*

The first step in UDL-based design is to consider how to create goals in specific, yet flexible ways. Ms. Takayama considered how to craft two goals that she had for all her students as they read Dr. King's story. She developed two standards-based goals, taking into account the variability of the language learners in the class. She derived her goals from key skills identified in the reading standards and came up with these two goals for this unit:

Students will be able to:

Goal I: Identify key events in Dr. King's life

Goal II: Identify which key events were challenges that he faced, and cite evidence from the text that shows how he persisted to meet his goals

Step 3: Assessments

Because **feedback and practice** are essential for language development, Ms. Takayama planned both formative and summative assessments throughout her instruction. Teachers commonly assess reading comprehension by having learners demonstrate their understanding through speaking or writing. If learners do not have the language to express their understanding, we may incorrectly determine that they do not understand. It is very common for early language learners to have more developed receptive than productive language, meaning that they can understand more than they can produce. Thus, Ms. Takayama considered how she could design flexible assessments, aligned with UDL guidelines, that would allow her students to demonstrate their comprehension more accurately and in a more engaging way.

Assessment for Goal 1

To demonstrate their ability to identify key events in Dr. King's life, Ms. Takayama had students develop a timeline. For all students, creating the timeline allowed them to chunk information and demonstrate their knowledge visually by labeling the sequence of events.

Ms. Takayama also varied the level of challenge in relation to students' language proficiency levels and **provided various options for generating language**:

- For the students who need the most support with language, she populated the timeline with dates and images and let the students complete the timeline with key missing details by putting in a corresponding word from a list of words that they had studied or by drawing a picture. She also provided **sentence frames** for slightly higher-level students to model complete sentences (e.g., "In _____ Martin Luther King Jr. began _____ at age 15." Students filled in *1944* and *college* in the blanks.

- For students who were long-term language learners (LTLLs), who typically have more developed verbal than written skills, she asked them to first tell a partner what they would include on their timeline template and then transfer those ideas into writing in complete sentences. She asked her higher-level students to set goals for how many sentences they would write about a sequence of events in Dr. King's life, and then create and complete their own timeline with images and sentences.

Assessment for Goal 2

During instruction, Ms. Takayama taught and reinforced the concepts required for finding evidence in the text. She created a formative assessment, which she had students do after teaching them how to find evidence. This formative assessment gave Ms. Takayama information on the level of understanding her learners had with the complex task of finding evidence, and helped her determine how much additional support individual students needed.

Ms. Takayama created small sticky notes (e.g., Post-it Notes) with various challenges and accomplishments of Dr. King's. She paired the students and asked them to categorize the sticky notes, identifying challenges and accomplishments and then finding evidence in the text to support each one. She circulated around the room assisting each pair in the process of finding evidence. After they completed the task, each pair could pick one challenge or accomplishment to present and describe the evidence they found.

After working in pairs, she further reinforced the concept with another similar assessment task. To do this, she provided students with a list of facts about Dr. King and had them identify which ones had evidence in the text and which did not. She then reinforced the concept that when they demonstrate understanding of reading, they must use the **evidence** from the text.

UDL Connections

Finding evidence pair activity (formative assessment): Use a grouping strategy to provide peer support, and opportunities for practice as a scaffold for individual learner demonstration of knowledge. (3.3 Guide information processing, visualization, and manipulation; 7.3 Minimize threats and distractions; 8.3 Foster collaboration and community)

Timeline (summative assessment): Support learners with various levels of scaffolds (e.g., images, sentence frames) and provide varying degrees of challenge to address learner

> **variability.** (3.3 Guide information processing, visualization, and manipulation; 6.3 Facilitate managing information and resources)

Step 4: Methods and Materials

After identifying her goals and the related assessments, Ms. Takayama considered how she could incorporate instructional strategies, activities, and formats (methods) and use resources and tools (materials) to provide supports and reduce barriers. She made instructional decisions related to each of the barriers she identified, the need to engage students, and their preferences.

Text Preview

Addressing barriers related to reading comprehension: Accessing Texts, Context, and Background

Because access to text can be a barrier for students, Ms. Takayama considered ways to address this barrier by **making input comprehensible.** On the first day of this unit, Ms. Takayama started with a preview of the text. She provided specific scaffolds to increase comprehension before she began reading the new text to the class. She considered the need for students to have information on the **context and background** of what they are reading.

In addition to the context, Ms. Takayama knew that some of her LLs' **background knowledge** did not align with the assumed and expected background knowledge necessary to access her text. The non-fiction text about Martin Luther King Jr. assumes knowledge of United States history, race relations, and civil rights. If LLs are unfamiliar with this history, understanding the text will be extremely challenging. Also, topics such as this can be very difficult for LLs to understand at all if they do not have a similar history, so using visuals and video clips to facilitate the background building can provide necessary support. Teachers can also activate their learners' background knowledge by making relatively abstract concepts (like *civil rights*) more concrete for students. For example, having students consider what rights people can and should have in their home countries can activate their background knowledge and make connections to conceptual similarities, which can aid in their comprehension.

Because of the difficulty many LLs may have understanding the context of Dr. King's era, and thus his life, Ms. Takayama began by showing signs that depicted segregation (e.g., segregated bathrooms and water fountains) and a brief clip from the movie, *Selma*, to help students understand the background. She then had the students gather in a circle to activate background by previewing **the chapter headings, subheadings, and other text features** while they followed along with their copies. This provided support by giving them an idea of the overall focus of the chapter. During this process, she created a large graphic organizer on the white board and wrote in the subheadings, which students copied into their two-column notes. Two-column notes help students organize information with space for students to write the big ideas on the left side and details on the right side. She also highlighted and posted key vocabulary words that they encountered in the preview. She then read the text aloud while students followed along on their copies.

UDL Connections

Provide information about the content in varied ways, explicitly highlighting key ideas. (3.1 Activate or supply background knowledge; 3.2 Highlight patterns, critical features, big ideas, and relationships)

Provide a graphic organizer. (3.2 Highlight patterns, critical features, big ideas, and relationships)

Provide background information that learners can relate to. (3.4 Maximize transfer and generalization)

Explicit and Contextualized Vocabulary Instruction

Addressing barriers related to reading comprehension: Vocabulary Knowledge

After the initial reading, she **built vocabulary knowledge** by **explicitly teaching the key vocabulary** that she had highlighted during their first reading of the text. She activated students' prior knowledge and asked them to rate how well they knew the word (i.e.,  know it well; know it, but not well enough to use it; or don't know it). She also asked them if they knew the word in their home language, and in some instances, they did. She made this activity more engaging for students by introducing each word separately and defining it, after which she asked the class for input and had them restate the definition in their own words. She listened to the definitions that the students came up with and **provided feedback, as needed,** to make the definitions concise and accurate. She also described how and when the word is used, reviewed the sentence from their text where the word appears, and provided an image to represent the word. She encouraged students to draw their own pictures to reinforce their understanding of the term. After introducing the vocabulary, each student chose one word that they would remember and teach to the class in upcoming days.

UDL Connections

Provide contextualized vocabulary instruction. (2.1 Clarify vocabulary and symbols)

Encourage learners to define words in home language. (2.4 Promote understanding across languages)

Use visuals to reinforce meanings of words. (2.5 Illustrate through multiple media)

Support learners to choose one word to define the next day. (7.1 Optimize individual choice and autonomy)

Reciprocal Teaching

Addressing engagement with reading: Sustained attention and reading

To address the issue of engagement, Ms. Takayama built in strategies that **support language production and interaction.** After previewing the text and studying the key vocabulary, Ms. Takayama's students were ready to read the text more deeply to identify the key details and evidence. She put students in groups of four and had them use an adaptation of the reciprocal teaching strategy (Brown & Palincsar, 1985) to scaffold and **support comprehension** of the text for each other. Together, they took out their two-column notes, where they wrote the main ideas on the left column and filled in details in the right column, from the preview of the chapter, as they read one section at a time. Ms. Takayama filled in the main ideas and included numbers to show the correct amount of details for her lower-level LLs.

Each student had a role:

* *Reader*: one student who can decode well reads a section of text out loud while others follow along

* *Questioner*: one student asks questions about the reading and other students respond (Ms. Takayama provided guiding questions for her LLs with lower levels of English proficiency)

* *Summarizer*: one student summarizes what the group understood from the reading, and other students add to the summary

* *Predictor*: one student uses the evidence to predict what they will learn in the next section of text, and other students agree or disagree

Ms. Takayama provided each of them with a description and sentence starters (e.g., "I predict that in the next section, we will learn . . .") to support their successful participation in this cooperative learning activity. As they went through this process with each section, they filled in their two-column notes with key words and evidence that they found. Newcomers in the groups **highlighted the key information in the text and drew pictures** in their notes to demonstrate their understanding.

After reading, students used their notes to discuss. Each group was assigned one section, and they worked together to decide what to fill in on the large graphic organizer that Ms. Takayama had drawn on the whiteboard. Each group got up and added what they learned to the class graphic organizer and then presented their section. Other groups participated by providing suggestions of what to add or revise, and in the process revised their own notes.

Ms. Takayama reminded the students of their goals, and asked them to review their notes and identify the evidence that they had found related to Dr. King's challenges and achievements. They highlighted challenges in yellow and achievements in green. They then worked together to transfer their key words and evidence into the timeline to deepen their understanding, noting the challenges and related achievements. This would lead into a future discussion related to how Dr. King persisted to meet his goals and contributed to the formative assessment related to citing evidence (practice and assessment for Goal 2 of this lesson).

UDL Connections

Use two-column notes, providing a structure and format for note-taking. (3.2 Highlight patterns, critical features, big ideas, and relationships, 3.3 Guide information processing, visualization, and manipulation)

Define clear roles when grouping learners. (6.3 Facilitate managing information and resources, 8.3 Foster collaboration and community)

> **Support learners to contribute to a whole class graphic organizer.** (3.3 Guide information processing, visualization, and manipulation)
>
> **Provide opportunities for practice and discussion of concepts in small group format.** (5.3 Build fluencies with graduated support for practice/performance, 7.3 Minimize threats and distractions)

Varied Formats and Digital Text

Addressing engagement with reading: sustained attention and reading

Ms. Takayama knew that her students faced a variety of barriers in **accessing grade-level texts**. Newcomers whose first languages use a different writing system can often face additional challenges with letter-sound correlation or symbol-sound cor- relation, which makes decoding and reading texts difficult. In middle school, this challenge is even more pronounced because phonics is no longer part of the standards and regular instruction. In addition to newcomers struggling to learn the writing system and decode texts, she also had LLs who could decode, but had limited fluency. This impeded their reading comprehension because they could not keep all of the information in their short-term memory for the length of time that it took them to slowly sound out each letter of each word and read the whole sentence. This resulted in a few students who could read but did not understand what they were reading. She also had LTLLs, who struggled with reading because they had learned the majority of the language that they knew aurally, and as a result, often did not recognize the written form of words that they actually did know. In order to meet these varied needs, as well as students' preferences, she provided options for how they read the text and **varied formats of texts** as well as opportunities to select their own texts.

After reading the text in their groups, Ms. Takayama gave students choices for reading the text one more time to build fluency and deepen their understanding. They had the option to stay with her and have her read aloud, or they could read independently with text-to-speech software, which provides valuable support for students who struggle with decoding (letter-sound correlation), fluency, and recognizing the written form of words. After reading the text through one or two times with the **text-to-speech support**, her students who struggled with decoding and fluency could then practice reading the text again independently, stopping to highlight and use text-to-speech support for any individual words that they forgot how to pronounce. Some of the texts also had vocabulary words with hyperlinked definitions to support students' understanding. This scaffolding can also build confidence and engage reluctant readers who feel that reading is an unpleasant task.

UDL Connections

Provide choices for reading formats. (7.1 Optimize individual choice and autonomy; 7.3 Minimize threats and distractions)

Show students how to use text-to-speech software and provide that as an option. (1.3 Offer alternatives for visual information; 4.2 Optimize access to tools and assistive technologies)

Independent Reading and Guided Choice

Addressing learner preferences and needs: relevance and learner interest

In addition to reading skills, Ms. Takayama focused on engagement when she introduced texts. She wanted to foster joy for reading with her students, and she knew that students can get frustrated when reading feels boring or like too much of a struggle. She included several components in her lesson to **support engagement and connection to reading**. She had a 10-minute daily independent reading time when students could find a cozy space and read. Many of her students chose to sit in bean-bag chairs and on the carpets that she had placed in one area of the classroom.

She knew her students loved to make their own choices. However, she realized that giving students open-ended choices on what to read can be tricky. Students may not be able to discern what is of interest to them or what books are at an appropriate level of challenge. Therefore, Ms. Takayama selected books at different reading levels and gave students **guided choices**. Knowing the instructional level that each student needed, she had them pick from three to five books she had selected. She knew that one of her new arrivals might be shy and unsure of expectations when she gave him choices. Because he had limited experiences with reading, he was unsure of what was expected and uncomfortable with making a selection. For him, Ms. Takayama selected three books and helped him make a choice. She pointed out pictures on the book cover and asked him what looked interesting to him. In addition to **supporting their choice of texts**, she allowed students to utilize the **varied formats** that she had taught them, such as text-to-speech, during their independent reading time. Many of her reluctant readers began to enjoy reading and felt more confident about their ability to comprehend and participate in class due to these flexible supports.

UDL Connections

Allow learners to make choices with selected books. (7.1 Optimize individual choice and autonomy)

Provide one-to-one support for specific learners who may need more assistance with choices. (8.4 Increase mastery-oriented feedback, 9.2 Facilitate personal coping skills and strategies)

Select books with themes that appeal to learners. (7.2 Optimize relevance, value, and authenticity)

IN SUMMARY: UDL-BASED LESSON DESIGN

The table below provides an overview of all the instructional planning decisions that Ms. Takayama made as she designed this lesson with UDL. Teachers can create and use a table like this to organize their ideas and then transfer them to any lesson planning format of their choice.

UDL DESIGN CONSIDERATIONS	IDEAS TO USE IN A LESSON PLAN
Step 1: Consider barriers, preferences, and support needs to address	1. Decoding 2. Fluency 3. Comprehension 4. Sustained attention to instruction and reading
Step 2: Goals	Grade-level standards • Cite textual evidence to support analysis of what the text says explicitly as well as inferences drawn from the text. • Determine a central idea of a text and how it is conveyed through particular details; provide a summary of the text distinct from personal opinions or judgments. Specific and flexible goals aligned with UDL: Goal 1: Identify key events in Dr. King's life Goal 2: Identify which key events were challenges that he faced and cite evidence from the text that shows how he persisted to meet his goals
Step 3: Assessments	Goal 1: Timeline (summative assessment) Goal 2: Finding evidence pair activity (formative assessment)

UDL DESIGN CONSIDERATIONS	IDEAS TO USE IN A LESSON PLAN
Step 4: Methods	Text Preview • Context provided for the reading • Background building and connections to prior knowledge using visuals, video, and providing examples that students may relate to • Graphic organizers or guided note-taking sheets to help focus LLs on what information they need to look for and find in the text Explicit and Contextualized vocabulary instruction • Active discussion of vocabulary words with whole class • Vocabulary discussion with connections to home language, using visuals, and drawing pictures to engage students Reciprocal Teaching • Collaborative strategy in which students have roles and active engagement in the reading process Varied Formats and Digital Text • Choice of reading independently or with the teacher • Text-to-speech option supporting new-comers' decoding and fluency and helping LTLLs to recognize words in print that they have heard, but don't know how to spell Independent reading and guided choice • Guided choices to facilitate students making connections • Culturally relevant and interesting texts

UDL DESIGN CONSIDERATIONS	IDEAS TO USE IN A LESSON PLAN
Step 4: Materials	Text Preview • Electronic text so that learners can use text-to-speech support • Sentence frames and starters within the graphic organizer to support learners to complete them correctly

ADDITIONAL RESOURCES

Alternatives and Extensions

	Making input comprehensible	• Use additional video clips and visuals to build background. • Provide leveled texts (e.g., Achieve 3000) for newcomers to reduce some of the academic language and complexity. • Amplify leveled texts with added visuals and graphics.
	Supporting language production and interaction	• Rotate groups with built-in accountability to support engagement and provide support. • Provide visuals for low-level learners to copy onto their timelines and label instead of writing sentences. • Extension activity: Ms. Takayama asks them to think about famous or historical figures that they know of from their own culture who faced challenges and persisted. Learners identify one challenge and one accomplishment related to this person, writes down or draws an image to depict this challenge and accomplishment, and then shares with the class or small group.

|  | Feed-back and practice | • Have learners with the same first language provide additional support to each other in their groups by explaining key concepts to each other in their first language before writing the words or sentences on their timelines. |

Connections to the Research Base

UDL-Culturally Responsive Teaching Connections

Gay, G. (2010). *Culturally responsive teaching: Theory, research, and practice.* New York, NY: Teachers College Press.

Reading Research

Fluency and Comprehension

Grabe, W. (2009). *Reading in a second language: moving from theory to practice.* Cambridge, NY: Cambridge University Press.

Jenkins, J. R., Fuchs, L. S., Broek, P. V., Espin, C., & Deno, S. L. (2003). Sources of individual differences in reading comprehension and reading fluency. *Journal of Educational Psychology, 95*(4), 719.

Wigfield, A., Guthrie, J. T., Perencevich, K. C., Taboada, A., Klauda, S. L., McRae, A., & Barbosa, P. (2008). Role of reading engagement in mediating effects of reading comprehension instruction on reading outcomes. *Psychology in the Schools, 45*(5), 432–445.

Purpose

Narvaez, D., Broek, P. V., & Ruiz, A. B. (1999). The influence of reading purpose on inference generation and comprehension in reading. *Journal of Educational Psychology, 91*(3), 488.

Noji, F., Ford, S., & Silva, A. (2009). Purposeful reading. In R. Cohen (Ed.), *Explorations in second language reading* (pp. 7–24). Alexandria, VA: Teachers of English to Speakers of Other Languages.

Pichert, J. W., & Anderson, R. C. (1977). Taking different perspectives on a story. *Journal of Educational Psychology, 69*(4), 309.

Vocabulary and Building Background

Anthony, A. R. (2008). Output Strategies for English-Language Learners: Theory to Practice. *The Reading Teacher, 61*(6), 472–482.

Marzano, R. J. (2004). *Building background knowledge for academic achievement: Research on what works in schools.* Alexandria, VA: Association for Supervision and Curriculum Development.

Nagy, W., & Townsend, D. (2012). Words as tools: Learning academic vocabulary as language acquisition. *Reading Research Quarterly, 47*(1), 91–108.

Scaffolding: Structured Progression of Learning, Peer Support, Reciprocal Teaching, and Amplifying the Text

Brown, A. L., & Palincsar, A. S. (1985). *Reciprocal teaching of comprehension strategies: A natural history of one program for enhancing learning.* Champaign, IL: University of Illinois at Urbana-Champaign.

Walqui, A. (2006). Scaffolding instruction for English language learners: A conceptual framework. *International Journal of Bilingual Education and Bilingualism, 9*(2), 159–180.

Varied Formats: Text-to-Speech

Stetter, M. E., & Hughes, M. T. (2010). Computer-assisted instruction to enhance the reading comprehension of struggling readers: A review of the literature. *Journal of Special Education Technology, 25*(4), 1–16.

4

Developing Writing Across the Curriculum

- Sustained attention to and persistence in writing
- Ability and motivation to make meaningful revisions

Learners' Preferences and Needs

- Varied ways of producing writing (different methods to generate and organize ideas)
- Individual preferences for collaborative/independent learning

>> Classroom Vignette: Social Studies

Mr. Lopez's school has adopted a plan for "writing across the curriculum," ensuring that students are actively learning and practicing writing skills in all content area classes. Mr. Lopez thought about the learner variability in his 11th grade social studies class and the challenges that posed for him with writing instruction. The class includes LLs, students with disabilities, and students who are in the gifted and talented program. Some students need additional writing instruction, some students benefit from support in various phases of writing (e.g., organizing thoughts before drafting), and all students can use writing practice at their levels of ability.

He is familiar with using UDL and culturally responsive strategies to support his students' reading comprehension and content understanding. He decided to apply his knowledge about UDL and culturally responsive strategies to writing, integrating supports that could be useful for his students who have such varied literacy skills and learning needs.

- 11th grade social studies
- 1 general education teacher
- 33 students
- Countries of birth:

    21 USA, 4 Pacific Island Countries (3 Chuuk, 1 Marshall Islands), 5 The Philippines, 1 Vietnam, 2 China

- Language learner variability:
    - 2 newcomers
    - 6 lived in the country 1–3 years, 2 with interrupted formal schooling
    - 4 LTLLs 5+ years in the country
- Other Learner Variability
    - 2 students identified with specific learning disability (SLD)
    - 80% of the students receiving free and reduced lunch
    - 3 students in the gifted and talented program

THE UDL DESIGN CYCLE: PLANNING A LESSON ON WRITING IN SOCIAL STUDIES

Mr. Lopez designed a lesson that integrates writing instruction with social studies content. In the following sections, we describe how he planned and designed the lesson using the UDL Design Cycle (detailed in Chapter 1). The UDL-based Lesson Summary (at the end of this chapter) provides an overview of how he applied UDL guidelines throughout his planning process.

Step 1: Identify Barriers, Preferences, and Support Needs

Mr. Lopez started by reflecting on the learner variability in his 11th grade class. He considered the varied needs of LLs who have differing language proficiency levels and the objectives in the individual education plans (IEPs) for the students with learning disabilities in order to identify some specific barriers that arise for students when they are faced with a writing task. In addition to reflecting on the barriers, he thought about students' preferences to determine what would engage them and help them persist with writing,

Barriers Related to Writing in Content Areas

Accessing texts and understanding content standards

- Foundational Reading Skills: Decoding and fluency
- Vocabulary knowledge
- In-depth, complex content standards

One major barrier to content understanding in social studies is **access to the text**. Particularly at the high school level, social studies textbooks can pose a challenge for struggling learners like LLs and students with disabilities because of the **dense and complex content**, which includes **academic and content-specific vocabulary**. If students cannot comprehend the content, they will lack the prerequisite knowledge needed to write about a particular topic. This poses a challenge for content area teachers, especially at a secondary level, who find they also need to be able to teach more **foundational reading** and writing skills for their increasing numbers of LLs, as well as their students with disabilities and struggling learners. In addition, research shows that some students living in poverty may experience additional challenges with cognitive functions that underlie literacy skill-building, including difficulty with reading comprehension and short-term memory (Korenman, Miller, & Sjaastad, 1995).

Providing explicit instruction on social studies–related vocabulary in context, graphic organizers and multimedia to support comprehension, and peer support are effective ways to support comprehension in content areas like social studies (Brown, 2007; Vaughn, et al., 2009). In fact, explicit and contextualized vocabulary instruction has been shown to support language development and content understanding, especially in social studies (Marzano, 2004).

In addition, students may not automatically recognize and understand the structure of academic texts in their second language (Ferris, 2009), which can create an additional barrier to accessing and understanding them. Because students cannot write about something that they do not understand, it is essential for teachers to support students' content knowledge and comprehension prior to expecting students to demonstrate understanding, especially through writing, which already poses a challenge.

General Barriers to Writing

Barriers to writing include challenges with all of the following:

- Generation of key ideas to demonstrate understanding in writing
- Organization of ideas
- Development of ideas—Generation of language without plagiarizing (vocabulary, grammar, syntax)
- Knowledge of writing conventions and genre (expectations)
- Sustained attention to and persistence in writing
- Ability and motivation to make meaningful revisions

Generating and organizing ideas for writing are typical challenges for struggling writers (Baker, Chard, Ketterlin-Geller, Apichatabutra, &

Doabler, 2009; Englert & Raphael, 1988), and LLs are no exception. A necessary first step to generating ideas in writing is planning and thinking about how to address the topic, which LLs typically struggle with. This also results in fewer ideas generated or included in their writing (Silva, 1996). In addition, synthesizing and summarizing information from academic texts is a challenging requirement, which is even harder for LLs than it is for their fluent classmates (Grabe & Zhang, 2013). Another challenge for LLs is that they often lack sufficient vocabulary to be able to summarize and paraphrase academic information well (Grabe & Zhange, 2013). This limited vocabulary also hinders language learners' abilities to **develop their ideas sufficiently**. Teachers often have expectations that students' writing will include well-developed and detailed summaries or analyses; however, developing and describing ideas requires extensive vocabulary, as well as varied grammatical structures, which many language learners may lack.

In addition to the linguistic challenges of summarizing and **paraphrasing** information, the concept of plagiarism can vary across cultures (Shi, 2006). Students may understand the concept, but due to differing cultural norms, they may face challenges in understanding how to appropriately utilize sources in academic writing in a second language and culture. Also, the requirements for different **genres of writing vary culturally** (Connor, 1996). Thus, LLs' writing may seem to be unorganized or lack cohesion because they are using typical organizational patterns for their first language.

For language learners, as well as many struggling learners, the complex processes involved in writing can make it hard to **sustain effort**. This is especially true for students who have not regularly experienced success in writing. Sustained effort is also required for students to proofread and revise after they finish writing, and unskilled and second language writers typically proofread and **revise** their writing less frequently and less effectively (Graham, Schwartz, & MacArthur, 1993; Porte, 1997) also leading to lower quality writing. This is in part because they do not know how to edit their own work effectively and because often they struggle to sustain the attention and motivation to review and revise what they have written.

Learners' Preferences and Needs

- Varied ways of producing writing (different methods to generate and organize ideas)
- Individual preferences for collaborative/independent learning

Students from diverse cultural and language backgrounds will often perceive information and academic demands and cognitive tasks differently (Ogbu, 1992). As a result, it is essential that teachers take this into account and provide flexible options for organizing information and **varied ways to produce writing,** rather than requiring all students to use one method of planning or specific format of graphic organizer.

Collaboration has been shown to support culturally and linguistically diverse students (CREDE, 2004; CREDE, 2015), and this is even more helpful in writing instruction because students' combined linguistic knowledge is much greater than their individual knowledge, so they can support each other's language development. Some students may like to work in groups and perform better collectively (Jordan, 1995), preferring that to organizing information individually. At the same time, it is important to keep in mind that some students may have a personal preference to learn and practice skills independently. Teachers should consider identifying their students' **personal and cultural preferences** for collaborative learning and provide varied opportunities for classroom activities to ensure that students have opportunities to engage in both modes (individual and collaborative) in ways that support their learning.

Step 2: Goals

Mr. Lopez used a textbook adopted by the 11th grade team as the basis for a lesson on World War 1. He developed a lesson that addresses two standards: a grade-level social studies standard (based on a state standard) and a Common Core State Standard (CCSS) related to writing in content areas.

Grade-level standard: Describe the role of secret alliances and nationalism in triggering the outbreak of World War I and the effort to prevent future wars by the establishment of the League of Nations. *(Based on the Hawaii State Content and Performance Standard for Social Studies SS.11.3.10)*

Writing in the Content Area Standard Write informative/explanatory texts, including the narration of historical events, scientific procedures/ experiments, or technical processes. *(Based on the Common Core State Standard for Literacy in History/ Social Studies, Science, and Technical Subjects WHST.11.2)*

Mr. Lopez carefully crafted two goals that are aligned to the two standards on which the lesson was based. He ensured that the goals were specific yet flexible, to give varied learners ways to reach mastery. Mr. Lopez reviewed the IEPs of the students with disabilities in his class to ensure that his goal statements allowed him to provide supports that address their IEP objectives, through flexible strategies and specific modifications and accommodations that they require.

Students will be able to:

- **Goal 1:** Describe in detail one of the main causes of World War I using a multimedia format.

- **Goal 2:** Write an informative essay describing how alliances and nationalism caused World War I and what the final trigger was for the war.

  - Goal 1 aligned to IEP: Student will write a total of 3 paragraphs with 5–7 sentences each when provided with an outline with sentence starters.

  - Goal 2 aligned to IEP: Student will make at least 3 revisions to writing after receiving teacher feedback.

Step 3: Assessments

Students were assessed on their content knowledge as well as their ability to express those ideas clearly in writing in alignment with the standards and goals. However, due to the learner variability in his class and the challenges that many of his students faced with both reading and writing, Mr. Lopez provided flexible assessments with varying levels of cognitive demands to support his students. He varied the demands and integrated options to ensure that LLs at all levels as well as his students with disabilities and those in the gifted and talented program were appropriately challenged.

Assessment for Goal 1: Students will collaborate to create and present a multimedia presentation detailing the main causes for World War I.

Assessment for Goal 2: Students will independently write an informative essay demonstrating their understanding of how nationalism, alliances, and the assassination of Archduke Ferdinand of Austria caused World War I.

Newcomers and LLs with very limited proficiency will complete sentence frames to demonstrate understanding of the two main causes and the one event that ultimately triggered the war.

UDL Connections

Multimedia Presentation (Formative assessment): Group students to create a multimedia presentation, with each group focusing on one subtopic. (5.1 Use multiple media for communication, 6.3 Facilitate managing information and resources; 7.3 Minimize threats and distractions; 8.3 Foster collaboration and community)

Essay (Summative assessment): Provide various scaffolds as students generate writing to help students with the conventions of writing and mastery of content required to successfully complete this assessment. To support variability of LLs, provide additional supports for newcomers and LLs with limited proficiency (e.g., sentence frames). In this example, the teacher wanted students to produce a written essay so the format was not flexible; however, he provided various supports and scaffolds (see Step 4 section below) to help students generate

ideas and express them in written format. (3.3 Guide information processing, visualization, and manipulation; 5.2 Use multiple
tools for construction and composition; 5.3 Build fluencies with
graduated levels of support for practice and performance; 6.2
Support planning and strategy development)

Step 4: Methods and Materials

As he planned the lesson, Mr. Lopez built in strategies to address
the barriers he had identified. He decided to start the lesson by integrating strategies to help students generate and organize ideas. He
also clarified the genre expectations for informational writing and
supported students in developing those ideas without plagiarizing.
Additionally, he used student choice and goal setting to help them
sustain engagement and effort as they wrote. Finally, he taught the
students a process to revise their writing and help them become more
independently proficient writers.

Collaborative Grouping Strategy

Addressing barriers related to writing: Generation and organi-
zation of ideas

To help students generate ideas, Mr. Lopez
decided to use a collaborative grouping strategy,
which allowed students to learn with and from peers
and better persist with the task. He considered how to intentionally
design groups to support the needs of his varied students. He created
groups of three, knowing that students would have more individual
accountability and opportunities to participate if the groups were not
too large. To **provide support for language production and interaction**, he grouped the students based on his knowledge of their literacy
skills and taking into consideration their personalities and preferences.
He ensured that students who needed additional supports for writing
were with other LLs who speak the same language (when possible).
He also tried to put one student who had more advanced writing skills

in each group. He put his two students who were proficient writers in groups thoughtfully, placing them with peers they were likely to collaborate well with and support. He avoided pairing his highest achieving and lowest achieving students because the large difference in ability can cause frustration.

Before they began the collaborative activity, he went over the **guidelines for collaboration** and specific role that each student would have in the group. His collaboration guidelines were to 1) participate actively, 2) listen to each other, and 3) help your peers. Each group was tasked with exploring one cause of WWI. He created 11 groups with three students each: four groups explored nationalism, four groups explored alliances, and three groups explored the assassination of Ferdinand (which he identified as the ultimate trigger of the war).

Resource Bank

Addressing barriers related to writing: Generation and organization of ideas

Before they began the group activity, students had already read the textbook together and had taken guided notes. Mr. Lopez **clarified the expectations** for the activity, which were to 1) share information and determine what the most important and relevant details are and 2) find information in a few related resources to add to their presentation. To **build academic background knowledge** needed for the activity, Mr. Lopez provided additional resources.

Before teaching this lesson, Mr. Lopez had put together an online "resource bank" for this activity to help guide students as they researched their topic independently and in their groups. He created a simple website (easily created using Google Sites or Weebly) with one page dedicated to each cause. On each page, he had identified three to five resources, including links for websites that have credible information and written in a way that **the input is comprehensible** for high school students. Each group only focused on the page with the information related to the cause they were assigned. Mr. Lopez showed the resource bank website to the whole class before they began using it, and provided an overview of the types of resources there were and what the student groups were supposed to do with them, noting that they could read information and cite the resource (a skill he has taught in a prior social studies lesson). As he did the demonstration, he showed students how they could activate the **text-to-speech feature** of the computer to listen and read the resources concurrently if they wished.

Writing in a Multimedia Environment

Addressing barriers related to writing: Organization and development of ideas

Mr. Lopez used a multimedia environment as a **scaffold to develop writing skills**. In the past, he had used readily available multimedia software (e.g., Google Slides, Open Office Impress, and Microsoft PowerPoint) to guide students through the pre-writing process of organizing information. The features of the software allowed students to "chunk" their ideas on slides and rearrange and organize the slides as needed. Although some students were proficient with organizing their thoughts before writing, many students benefitted from practice with organizing what they would write and outlining prior to drafting a text. He knew that information is organized differently in many of his LLs' first languages, and that his students with specific learning disabilities (SLD) also often struggled to organize their thoughts in writing. In addition, Mr. Lopez also had many students who struggled with reading comprehension and short-term memory deficits, so he **chunked the tasks** to support his students' organization skills and memory.

Mr. Lopez used Google Slides for this activity because it is free and available on all the classroom computers (note: this activity can be done in other multimedia software such as Open Office Impress, Microsoft PowerPoint, or Apple Keynote). He created a template in Google Slides with five slides that had headers noting what students should include. He created a paper-based graphic organizer with the same headers so that students could take notes on paper when they first talked in their groups.

In addition to **modeling how information could be organized**, the template also provided a guide for the group discussion. Students can struggle with the abstract and unstructured nature of open-ended group discussions, especially when there are varied levels of comprehension on a complex topic. Mr. Lopez modeled with the whole class how they could use the headers on each slide as a starting point for what to discuss in their groups. To ensure that groups also had autonomy and choices with organizing information, Mr. Lopez noted that they could be creative and reorganize slides if they preferred to address topics in a different way. He let students know that he would be walking around and listening in on group discussions and could give feedback on different ideas for organization.

Mr. Lopez provided clear expectations of what the groups should accomplish in the two class periods dedicated to this activity. Each student was provided with a **checklist of what elements needed to be included**, and the groups used those collaboratively to determine if they were including all of the required elements. As he walked around and checked in with groups, Mr. Lopez also provided sentence starters for his lower level LLs to help them feel confident about participating in the group project.

Mr. Lopez had a one-to-one conference with each group as they finalized their Google Slides. This allowed him to **provide mastery-oriented feedback** to help groups meet objectives. Each group reported on how they had met all elements of the checklist,  and Mr. Lopez was able to give specific and targeted feedback on areas they could strengthen. Students then had the **opportunity to use the feedback to revise** their presentations based on discussion and feedback. These one-on-one group conferences also gave Mr. Lopez a way to discuss the slides with all students and ask questions to make sure every student had something they could articulate about the content on the slides. Students who were not proficient with writing and literacy skills were able to verbally articulate their understanding of their topic to Mr. Lopez and prepare for the next activity.

After each group had revised their slides, Mr. Lopez used a "jigsaw strategy," regrouping students into new groups that included one "expert" on each topic from the original groups. This allowed the students to share what they had learned in a small group, and reduced anxiety for some students who might feel overwhelmed or nervous to present in front of the whole class. Building their expertise and fluency about a topic in their original group also **reduced anxiety and increased confidence** in explaining the topic for students who were at varied levels of oral language proficiency. As students presented, their classmates took notes about the key information and details, so that they could include them in the next step.

UDL Connections

Be strategic about group work. Think about how to formulate student groups, taking into account literacy learning levels, needs, and characteristics of group members, including socioemotional factors like reducing anxiety and building confidence to use oral language. (8.3 Foster collaboration and community)

Provide structure for student discussion and create a template to provide a guide as students engage with complex content. (3.2 Highlight patterns, critical features, big ideas, and relationships; 5.1 Use multiple tools for construction and composition; 6.2 Support planning and strategy development)

Use multimodal environments (e.g., presentation software) for the creation and expression of knowledge. This can provide structure for organization and planning and help to break tasks down. (4.2 Optimize access to tools and assistive technologies; 5.1 Multiple media for communication)

> Have one-to-one conferences to provide timely feedback and support students who can benefit from guided opportunities to use and practice language. (8.3 provide mastery-oriented feedback; 9.1 Promote expectations and beliefs that optimize motivation)

Mini-Lesson: Writing in Your Own Words

Addressing barriers to writing: Development of ideas without plagiarizing (vocabulary, grammar, syntax)

Mr. Lopez incorporated a mini-lesson on plagiarism, knowing he could reinforce this important concept in the context of using the resource bank for their group activity. He started by clearly identifying the purpose of the mini-lesson. He reminded students that for all writing assignments, plagiarism is an important consideration. He also defined plagiarism in more direct terms to ensure that students at various literacy levels and from different cultures with different definitions of plagiarism could understand the core concept. He noted that students should represent other people's ideas in their own words and credit the source of those ideas.

He made this mini-lesson fun for the students by giving them the opportunity to demonstrate what they should not do and then follow up with what they should do. He modeled this first with one text in the resource bank. He copied and pasted a passage and asked students if that was okay, and when they all agreed that that was plagiarism, he asked them what they could do instead. He used this opportunity to reinforce some rules for paraphrasing as he **modeled how to properly use ideas from sources in writing:**

1. **Reread** the original passage until you understand its full meaning.
2. **Cover** the original, so that you don't copy any words or phrases and **write** the idea in your own words.

3. **Check** your paraphrasing to ensure that:
   - you did not change the meaning
   - you did not copy the original (words or structure!)

After modeling this with the whole class, he selected pairs of students to come up and try it. He was thoughtful about the pairs, ensuring that students who needed support with the process were paired with students who were more proficient with literacy skills. He was also mindful that some students would not be ready to come up and do the activity in front of the class, so he made sure not to put them on the spot, knowing that language and learning do not develop well when students, particularly language learners, feel high levels of anxiety.

He had three pairs come up and model "The Bad" (plagiarizing) and "The Good" (paraphrasing and citing) with various resources they selected from the resource bank. Students enjoyed the activity, laughing at the "bad" copying and helping their peers with paraphrasing. In this way, all students saw **the process of paraphrasing being made explicit**, and it demystified both the process and the expectation of "writing in your own words."

Models and Exemplars Discussion

Addressing barriers to writing: knowledge of writing conventions and genre (expectations)

The whole class activity was designed to give students some support and scaffolding and **to provide support for language production** before they wrote independently. To help students transfer that infor-  mation and successfully undertake an independent writing assignment, Mr. Lopez started by **reinforcing expectations** for a written essay and reminding them about the structure for the genre of informative writing. He began by explaining what informative writing is and giving the students a few examples of informational texts that they had read in his and other classes. Then, he asked the students to share other informational texts that they had read and what the purpose was of those texts.

Using an exemplar that he had from a prior year, Mr. Lopez had his students "grade" an essay together. He handed out a printed copy of the essay to all students and projected it on the screen. He asked them to focus on various parts of the essay (e.g., introduction, topic sentences, evidence), and they assessed each part. He showed the students how the essay included an introduction that clearly stated the topic.

He noted how each paragraph had a clear focus with a topic sentence, and sentences that developed the idea with evidence. He highlighted the topic sentence on screen and asked the students to find and  highlight topic sentences throughout the essay on their printed copies. He continued this process of discussing the components of an essay with the class, using the example to make his points. During this discussion, Mr. Lopez asked targeted questions, guiding students to identify strengths and weaknesses in the essay. Students enjoyed being able to grade and give feedback on areas they considered strong and weak. The activity also **actively fostered interactions** in the target language. For the students who were less proficient with writing skills, he provided scaffolds. For example, after the class highlighted an area of the essay, he called on specific students to restate what the area was, providing additional sentence starters for his LLs (e.g., "The topic sentence is...").

Throughout this process, Mr. Lopez reiterated for the students that the purpose of analyzing and deconstructing this essay was to model for them how they should structure the assignment that they were about to write. After grading the essay together as a class, he provided each student with a guided outline. This outline had prompts for each paragraph that the students needed to write to remind them to introduce the essay by clearly describing the topic and then to introduce each of the ideas with a topic sentence. He reminded them that each topic also should have one clear focus and supporting details, which was also noted on the outline. Finally, the outline included an area for a conclusion with a final message.

UDL Connections

Provide explicit instruction and modeling on expectations of structure and format. (2.2 Clarify syntax and structure; 3.1 Activate or supply background knowledge; 6.2 Support planning and strategy development)

Engage students in discussion about expectations in an authentic way (e.g., analyzing an exemplar together). (3.4 Maximize transfer and generalization; 6.4 Enhance capacity of monitoring progress)

Give students opportunities to use academic language about what is expected (in this case, the conventions of writing). Provide multiple options for viewing and discussing the content and skills. (2.4 Promote understanding across languages)

Self-Regulation Strategies

Addressing barriers to writing: Sustained attention to and persistence with writing

Mr. Lopez knew that many of his students, in particular his LLs and students with disabilities, struggled to persist when challenges with writing arose. He used the outline that all students had as an additional scaffold for the struggling writers. For specific students, he set targets for specific areas, chunking down the larger and more daunting task of writing a whole essay. He also addressed the IEP goal of one of his students by writing down the number of sentences that were supposed to be included in each part of the outline and resulting essay. When they finished that part of the outline, they brought it to him for **feedback**. In this way, he gave students the support to write one paragraph at a time. The students used the outline as a checklist, **monitoring their own progress** and stopping at each section to ensure that they had included the necessary information.

Knowing that some students, including a few LLs and one of the students with a learning disability, disliked handwriting, he gave students the option to use the classroom laptops to type the outlines and their

essays. Many of his students, including several LLs, preferred to use the computers because the mechanics of handwriting were challenging for them and because the built-in spellcheck and grammar check helped them to edit their own writing. One of his LLs, however, was a newcomer, who had not used computers before and was not confident with technology, so he did not require the students to type the essay; he just provided it as an **alternative option for writing format.** He also encouraged his LTLLs to say their ideas out loud and then write down what they heard themselves say in order to increase their fluency in writing and turning their ideas into sentences. He arranged a few desks on one side of the classroom for those students so that they did not feel self-conscious or disrupt other students who were trying to concentrate.

Several students had a hard time writing for a long period of time and would become distracted after sitting for too long trying to write. Mr. Lopez instated "writing breaks"; students were allowed one writing break during each class period. Mr. Lopez

asked students to identify a certain chunk of writing they would do on their checklist, and once they finished writing that part, they would bring it to Mr. Lopez and earn a 3-minute break. As he looked over the piece, students could take their three-minute break by going to the back of the room where the computers were. Students could choose how they wanted to use this break. Some students put on headphones and listened to a song, and others surfed the web for a few minutes. One stipulation was that they had to take their break quietly and without disrupting anyone else to continue earning breaks in the future. By letting students set their own targets for the break, Mr. Lopez was able to help students at their own levels, giving appropriate and **just-in-time feedback** on various areas of their writing. These breaks reduced some of the behavioral issues that had come up during independent writing tasks in the past when students got distracted and disruptive to others.

UDL Connections

Provide ways for students to manage time and chunk their tasks into manageable pieces. (7.3 Minimize threats and distractions; 9.2 Facilitate personal coping skills and strategies)

Provide structure with specific milestones for progress. (6.1 Guide appropriate goal setting)

Use technology and tools that support students as they learn and express information. (4.2 Optimize access to tools and assistive technologies)

Mini-Lesson: Review Skills

Addressing barriers to writing: Ability and motivation to make meaningful revisions

Because language learners and students with disabilities are typically less effective at revising, and in fact even attempt it less, after providing feedback on each student's writing, Mr. Lopez integrated a mini-lesson with **explicit instruction on how to revise** **effectively.** Within this mini-lesson he included language development instruction for those students who needed extra literacy support. He addressed two areas in this mini-lesson: 1) he gave students a structured way of reviewing their essays to look for various components they should have included and 2) he explained how they could proofread their essays with a specific goal in mind.

The students used the classroom laptops for their revisions. For most students, revising on the computers made editing less tedious because they could use various features as they edited, such as copying and pasting. Mr. Lopez reminded them of the lesson they did when they highlighted key parts of the exemplar essay in class. He asked students to look first at their individual checklists and review their outlines to see if they were missing any of the components. They used the computer to highlight their topic sentences in yellow and their evidence in blue. If they found that they were missing anything, they were encouraged to check with Mr. Lopez on how to develop a specific area. In this way, Mr. Lopez gave students the opportunity to assess their own written text with specific guidance on what to look for.

Mr. Lopez knew that some of the LLs in his class struggled with basic grammar. Because writing about World War I requires extensive use of the past tense, Mr. Lopez provided **explicit grammar instruction** on the past tense to a small group of students. He modeled the correct form, showed a few examples of incorrect sentences, and had the students work together to correct the verb tenses in the sentences. He told the students that they would check their essays with the specific goal of reviewing verb tenses and finding any that were incorrect. He explained that picking one goal and then focusing on it is one way to make proofreading easier. When they revised their papers independently, they were supposed to also pick one focus and review the paper with that one focus in mind. After the students did their own review and revision, Mr. Lopez provided **specific feedback** on each student's overall writing and grammar. He avoided comments, like, "Great!" knowing that non-specific positive feedback is typically not helpful, and can actually have a detrimental effect on students' motivation to continue working. Instead, he provided feedback specific to his instruction, like, "Great job including a clear topic sentence in this paragraph."

By the end of the lessons, students felt more confident about their own writing ability because they saw how they could generate a whole essay in a step-by-step manner. Mr. Lopez reminded the students that they could use this strategy to help them with their writing in other classes, too.

UDL Connections

Provide explicit instruction, as needed, on component skills and specific areas of the learning process. This assistance can be provided to specific groups of students, as needed. (5.3 Build fluencies with graduated levels of support for practice and performance)

Provide specific goals for students as they undertake larger open-ended tasks. (7.3 Minimize threats and distractions; 8.1 Heighten salience of goals and objectives)

Support review and reflection and provide guidance on specific expectations. (9.1 Promote expectations and beliefs that optimize motivation)

IN SUMMARY: UDL-BASED LESSON DESIGN

The table below provides an overview of all the instructional planning decisions that Mr. Lopez made as he designed this lesson with UDL. Teachers can create and use a table like this to organize their ideas, and then transfer them to any lesson-planning format of their choice.

UDL DESIGN CONSIDERATIONS	IDEAS TO USE IN A LESSON PLAN
Step 1: Consider barriers, preferences, and support needs to address	1. Accessing Texts 2. Understanding writing conventions and genre expectations 3. Generating and organizing ideas 4. Developing Ideas 5. Sustaining writing 6. Revising writing

UDL DESIGN CONSIDERATIONS	IDEAS TO USE IN A LESSON PLAN
Step 2: Goals	Grade-level standards • Describe the roles of secret alliances and nationalism in triggering the outbreak of World War I, and the effort to prevent future wars by the establishment of the League of Nations. • Write informative and explanatory texts, including the narration of historical events, scientific procedures or experiments, or technical processes. Specific and flexible goals aligned with UDL: • Goal 1: Create a collaborative Google Slides presentation describing one of the causes of World War I. • Goal 2: Write an informative essay describing how alliances and nationalism caused World War I. • Goal 1 aligned to IEP: Student will write a total of three paragraphs with five to seven sentences each when provided with an outline with sentence starters. • Goal 2 aligned to IEP: Student will make at least three revisions to writing after receiving teacher feedback.
Step 3: Assessments	Goal 1: Multimedia presentation (formative assessment) Goal 2: Informative essay (summative assessment)

UDL DESIGN CONSIDERATIONS	IDEAS TO USE IN A LESSON PLAN
Step 4: Methods	Collaborative Grouping Strategy • Clear guidelines for how to collaborate with peers • Strategic groups with varied levels and same language partners • Opportunities for discussion and interaction to allow students to access their collective knowledge and language Resource Bank • Additional resources to build academic background • Opportunities for student choice in the sources of information that they include in their presentation and writing Writing in a Multimedia Environment • Pre-writing with guidance (chunk ideas, use visuals, add text, add audio recording) • Digital template with headers noting what students should include • Paper-based graphic organizer with the same headers to allow choice • Option for students to reorganize slides and outlines and be creative Mini-Lesson: Writing in Your Own Words • Targeted and specific instruction on how to write in their own words • Use of models to discuss concepts of paraphrasing vs plagiarizing

UDL DESIGN CONSIDERATIONS	IDEAS TO USE IN A LESSON PLAN
Step 4: Methods	Models and Exemplars Discussion • Oral presentation of ideas prior to writing • Modeling and guidance by teacher for students to label the parts of an exemplar essay Self-Regulation Strategy • Opportunities for feedback and additional practice embedded throughout all parts of the lesson, including individual conferences with the teacher • Essay writing in chunks with scheduled breaks to maintain motivation • Checklist for self-assessment Mini-Lesson: Review Skills • Targeted and specific language instruction on how to revise
Step 4: Materials	Flexible Materials • Template for organizing information in a multimedia environment (e.g., Google Slides) and on paper • Online sources to supplement the course text • Text-to-speech to read online sources • Sentence starters and frames for LLs • Students' notes from reading the class text, as well as from their classmates' oral presentations, to generate ideas for writing • Models and examples (e.g., plagiarism, student analysis to identify the good and bad examples in pairs) • Guided outline for writing and for students with related IEP goals, including the number of required ideas and sentences

ADDITIONAL RESOURCES

Alternatives and Extensions

	Making input comprehensible	• Provide sample texts that are already highlighted and annotated to support lower level LLs during the activity to identify parts of the essay. • Provide a word bank with useful vocabulary for LLs to use.
	Supporting language production and interaction	• Extension activity: Mr. Lopez asks them to think about current events and identify any tensions that could lead up to a third world war and what types of triggers could start it. • Extension activity: Students can choose to include a connection to a trigger in another war, and LLs can use knowledge that they have or that they learn from their families related to their home countries.
	Feedback and practice	• Have students use a list of transitional words to identify in the same sample text. They can then try to add appropriate transitional words in their own essays and give each other feedback on the transitional words that they included.

Connections to the Research Base

UDL-Culturally Responsive Teaching connections

Jordan, C. (1995). Creating cultures of schooling: Historical and conceptual background of the KEEP/Rough Rock collaboration. *Bilingual Research Journal, 19*(1), 83–100.

Cultural Differences in Writing

Connor, U. (1996). *Contrastive rhetoric: Cross-cultural aspects of second language writing.* New York, NY: Cambridge University Press.

Center for Research on Education, Diversity, & Excellence (CREDE). (2004). *Observing the five standards in practice: Development and application of the standards performance continuum.* Santa Cruz, CA: University of California.

Center for Research on Education, Diversity & Excellence (CREDE) Hawai'i Project. (2015). Retrieved April 19, 2014, from *http://manoa.hawaii.edu/coe/crede/*

Ogbu, J. U. (1992). Understanding cultural diversity and learning. *Educational researcher, 21*(8), 5–14.

Shi, L. (2006). Cultural backgrounds and textual appropriation. *Language Awareness, 15*(4), 264–282. doi:10.2167/la406.0

Supporting Language Learners in Content Areas, Social Studies

Brown, C. (2007). Strategies for making social studies texts more comprehensible for English-language learners. *The Social Studies, 98*(5), 185–188.

Vaughn, S., Martinez, L. R., Linan-Thompson, S., Reutebuch, C. K., Carlson, C. D., & Francis, D. J. (2009). Enhancing social studies vocabulary and comprehension for seventh-grade English language learners: Findings from two experimental studies. *Journal of Research on Educational Effectiveness, 2*(4), 297–324.

Vocabulary and Building Background

Marzano, R. J. (2004). *Building background knowledge for academic achievement: research on what works in schools.* Alexandria, VA: Association for Supervision and Curriculum Development.

Vaughn, S., Martinez, L. R., Linan-Thompson, S., Reutebuch, C. K., Carlson, C. D., & Francis, D. J. (2009). Enhancing social studies vocabulary and comprehension for seventh-grade English language learners: Findings from two experimental studies. *Journal of Research on Educational Effectiveness, 2*(4), 297-324.

Writing Instruction

Baker, S. K., Chard, D. J., Ketterlin-Geller, L. R., Apichatabutra, C., & Doabler, C. (2009). Teaching writing to at-risk students. The quality of evidence for Self-Regulated Strategy Development. *Exceptional Children, 75*(3), 303–318.

Grabe, W., & Zhang, C. (2013). Reading and writing together: A critical component of English for academic purposes teaching and learning. *TESOL Journal, 4*(1), 9–24.

Harris, K. & Graham, S. (1996). *Making the writing process work: Strategies for composition and self-regulation* (2nd ed.). Cambridge, MA: Brookline.

Harris, K., Graham, S., Mason, L., & Friedlander, B. (2008). *Powerful writing strategies for all students.* Baltimore, MA: Paul H. Brooks Publishing Co.

Mason, L. H., & Cramer, A. M. (2014). Linking classroom assessment to written language interventions. *Academic Assessment and Intervention*, 241.

Rouse, A. G., & Collins, A. A. (2016). Effective and Ineffective Writing Practices for Students with Disabilities. In *Instructional Practices with and without Empirical Validity* (pp. 61–84). Emerald Group Publishing Limited.

Characteristics of Student Writing

Graham, S. (2011). The process writing approach: A meta-analysis. *The Journal of Educational Research, 104*(6), 396–407.

Porte, G. K. (1997). The etiology of poor second language writing: The influence of perceived teacher preferences on second language revision strategies. *Journal of Second Language Writing, 6*(1), 61–78.

Silva, T. (1993). Toward an understanding of the distinct nature of L2 writing: The ESL research and its implications. *TESOL Quarterly, 27*(4), 657–677.

Poverty and Cognition

Korenman, S., Miller, J. E., & Sjaastad, J. E. (1995). Long-term poverty and child development in the United States: Results from the NLSY. *Children and Youth Services Review, 17*(1–2), 127–155.

5

Developing Vocabulary Across the Curriculum

Chapter at a Glance:

Using UDL to address the following barriers and learner preferences and needs:

Barriers Related to Math Instruction

- Vocabulary
- Cultural considerations
- Language of word problems
- Explaining and justifying answers

Learners' Preferences and Needs

- Varied formats for input (different methods to generate and organize ideas)
- Individual preferences

>> Classroom Vignette: Math

Mrs. Hooks designs her lessons with UDL to meet the needs of the diverse students across content areas in her third grade class. Over the past several years, the number of LLs in her classes has been steadily increasing, and many arrive with very limited proficiency in the language of instruction. For this reason, Mrs. Hooks decided to integrate more vocabulary into all of the subjects that she teaches, including math.

>> Classroom Profile

- 3rd grade math
- 1 general education teacher
- 24 students
- Countries of birth:

    12 USA, 7 Mexico, 2 El Salvador, 2 Vietnam, 1 Chuuk
- Language learner variability:
    - 4 newcomers
    - 8 lived in the country 1–3 years, 4 with interrupted formal schooling
- Other learner variability
    - 3 Students with learning disabilities (includes 1 LL)
    - 65% of the students receiving free and reduced lunch

THE UDL DESIGN CYCLE: PLANNING A MATH LESSON WITH A VOCABULARY FOCUS

Mrs. Hooks noticed that her students made gains in reading comprehension as well as mastery of content when she used focused vocabulary instruction strategies during her social studies lessons. Her third graders struggled in their math instruction block more than any of the other subjects, so she decided to include sustained vocabulary instruction in math as well to see if it would support her students' understanding and performance. Considering UDL Guideline 2: Provide options for language, mathematical expressions, and symbols, she decided to use the UDL Design cycle (see Chapter 1) to develop a math lesson with a focus on vocabulary instruction. In the following sections, we describe how she planned and designed a math lesson, taking UDL into consideration at the outset. The UDL-based lesson summary (at the end of this chapter) provides an overview of how she applied UDL throughout her planning process.

Step 1: Identify Barriers, Preferences, and Support Needs

Word problems, vocabulary, math concepts, cultural differences, and explaining and justifying their answers in math all pose significant challenges for LLs and struggling learners in math class. Before designing a lesson, Mrs. Hooks considered these barriers to teaching math content. This helped her determine what instructional strategies she would use for all students and ensure that she embedded the necessary accommodations for her students who had IEPs for specific disabilities.

Barriers Related to Math Instruction

- Vocabulary
- Cultural considerations
- Language of word problems
- Explaining and justifying answers

Vocabulary

Vocabulary knowledge is highly correlated with academic success (Nagy & Townsend, 2012), but language learners typically have limited vocabulary and much less vocabulary knowledge than their fluent peers, which negatively impacts their comprehension in school (Carlo et al., 2004). However, vocabulary development in context has been shown to result in significant increases in students' academic achievement (Marzano, 2001 & Marzano, 2004). Simply providing lists and definitions will not be sufficient to develop students' receptive and productive vocabulary knowledge and their academic achievement. Instead, they need to be taught the vocabulary in context, and then be provided with opportunities to encounter it in their texts and instructions and use it in order to fully learn it (Carlo et al., 2004).

Vocabulary in math instruction is particularly challenging for LLs because it is complex in nature. However, math is typically thought of as a universal language that is easier for LLs, so little attention has been paid to supporting language in math (Bransford, 2000).

Language use in math includes complexity that poses challenges for LLs (Ernst-Slavit & Slavit, 2007) in a variety of areas:

- **Multiple-meaning vocabulary** words that LLs may have developed conversationally may also occur in math with different meanings (e.g., *table* and *pie* [*pi*]).

- **Specialized, technical vocabulary** words that only occur in math (e.g., Pythagorean and numerator) need to be learned for LLs.

- **General academic vocabulary** words (e.g., compare and identify) may also cause barriers to LLs' understanding.

- **Prepositions** are typically very challenging for LLs to acquire, and in math, they have very specific meanings (e.g., 9 *divided by* 3 means 9÷3, but 9 *divided into* 3 represents 3÷9).

- **Complex phrases** often cannot be translated directly, so may cause confusion if LLs try to look up the meaning (e.g., *least common denominator*). Another type of complex phrase results because often there is not a direct correlation with the order of a sentence in math and its numerical representation (e.g., *x is 9* *more than y* is represented as x = 9 + y, but many learners expect it to be x + 9 = y).

- **Synonyms** are frequently used in math to represent the same operation (e.g., *add, plus, more than,* and others). In addition, word problems may also use synonyms to represent the same idea (e.g., Who *made* the highest points on the test if Eri *earned* 3 points, Esmerelda *scored* 5 plus an extra credit point, and Son *got* 4?).
- **Symbols** can also pose a challenge because many symbols can represent the same operation in math (e.g., multiplication of 9 and x can be represented as: 9x, x9, 9(x), x(9), 9•x, x•9).

Cultural Considerations

Students, and LLs in particular, need to activate prior knowledge and connect new learning to what they have already learned and experienced, and linking to students' cultures and first languages facilitates this process (Cummins, 2009). In addition, culturally relevant instruction highlights the need for learning to be contextualized within experiences that culturally and linguistically diverse learners can make connections to, and thus, better comprehend and internalize (CREDE, 2004; CREDE 2015). However, this is often not done in mathematics instruction. Students may be good at counting money and figuring out how many snacks they can buy at the corner store with the amount of change in their pockets, but fail when faced with a worksheet on decimals or place value. This is because the connection between what they know and are good at is not made in their math instruction. Making mathematics relevant to students' lives and connecting instruction to real-world experiences or real-world skills that they might already possess is essential for success and engagement in math, in particular for students who typically struggle with math more than their culturally mainstream peers.

Students' first languages are the foundation they can successfully connect with to understand new information (Garcia, 1995). In addition, the National Council of Teachers of Mathematics (2017) declares that teachers must be, "responsive to students' backgrounds, experiences, cultural perspectives, traditions, and knowledge when designing and implementing a mathematics program and assessing its effectiveness," (para. 1), and that this must also include high levels of rigor for all students.

To respond to and make sense of different environments, math has developed differently in different cultures (Rosa, 2015). Teachers must recognize and pay attention to the fact that students from different cultures may have developed math concepts differently; for example, the Haitian method of subtraction is performed in the opposite way that it is usually taught in the United States, by thinking about how many more they need to add to a number to reach the total, rather than taking away one number from another (Coyne, n.d.). In addition, people count differently in different languages. For example, in Japanese, the word *man* (pronounced: *mahn*) means 10,000, so Japanese people would say *five man* for 50,000, which means five ten thousand instead of fifty thousand in English and other Indo-European languages. This could impact the way that students count, organize, and conceptualize numbers, as well.

Language of Word Problems

In addition to complex vocabulary and cultural assumptions in math, word problems also pose challenges for LLs due to extra unnecessary information in the problem, assumed background knowledge, and vocabulary words that students do not know, which are unrelated to math and other academic subjects. Not surprisingly, LLs' reading comprehension impacts their ability to understand and solve word problems (Brown, 2005). In fact, research suggests that to clearly understand, readers must comprehend at least 90% of the words in a text (Nagy & Scott, 2000), so the longer and more complex a word problem is, the lower the likelihood that LLs will be able to understand clearly enough to solve it. Word problems also often include multiple steps that students have to decipher and organize before they can even begin to do the computation.

Explaining and Justifying Answers

The math standards and many newer standardized tests require students to explain and justify their answers in math. This poses additional difficulties for LLs because not only do they have to understand the math problem, possibly a word problem, and do the computation, but they also must write complete sentences to explain and justify their process of computation, which is a much bigger language demand. As a result, this is a bigger challenge for LLs (Abedi, 2004).

Learners' Preferences and Needs

* **Varied formats for production (different methods to generate and organize ideas)**
* **Individual preferences**

In addition to learning different procedures for math processes and different organizational patterns for numbers, the way that students organize information in general varies culturally (Ogbu, 1992). Thus, providing students a framework for how to organize math problems, but allowing students flexible options for how they want to organize the information can help support students in making sense of complex math computation and word problems. Allowing students to collaborate, share strategies, and help each other can also be an important support, because culturally, some students may learn better and feel more supported working in groups or pairs (CREDE, 2004; CREDE, 2015).

Step 2: Goals

The third grade teachers at Mrs. Hooks' school all use the same textbook; however, the section on comparing fractions and equivalent fractions does not provide in-depth explanations or extensive opportunities for practice. Thus, Mrs. Hooks always supplements the text with additional explanation and practice because she knows that fractions are a foundational concept that students typically struggle with. She planned a lesson using flexible materials and methods with multiple opportunities for feedback to address a grade-level math standard related to fractions.

Grade-Level Standard: Explain equivalence of fractions in special cases and compare fractions by reasoning about their size.

Recognize and generate simple equivalent fractions, e.g., $1/2 = 2/4$, $4/6 = 2/3$. Explain why the fractions are equivalent, e.g., by using a visual fraction model. *(Based on the Common Core State Standard for Math CCSS 3.NF.3)*

Mrs. Hooks began with the first stage in designing a lesson with UDL by developing goals that were specific and aligned to standards. She designed her goals to allow for some flexibility of expression. Mrs. Hooks also reviewed the IEPs of the students with disabilities in her class to ensure that she was also supporting their specific IEP goals and providing the necessary accommodations.

- **Goal 1:** Compare equivalent fractions using visual models.
- **Goal 2:** Explain in writing and demonstrate with a visual model why two fractions are equivalent.
- **Goal aligned to IEP:** Student will draw and label a picture with denominators provided to show two equivalent fractions.

Step 3: Assessments

Mrs. Hooks designed assessments that allowed students of varying levels of language proficiency to express what they learned during and at the end of the lesson. During the lesson, Mrs. Hooks chose to use a formative assessment to evaluate how students were progressing toward Goal 1. For this formative assessment, Mrs. Hooks decided to pair students with peers, matching a student who had greater proficiency with one who required more support with either math or language. For Goal 2, Mrs. Hooks developed a summative assessment of the core concepts, but provided scaffolds to help students express what they knew at their varied levels of language fluency.

Assessment for Goal 1: Students will work in groups to draw pictures of equivalent fractions.

Assessment for Goal 2: Students will draw a visual model and explain in writing to demonstrate understanding of equivalent fractions from a word problem.

- Newcomers will complete sentence frames (_____ is equivalent to _____ because_____.) to explain their visual models.

- Differentiation related to IEP goal: The student will be given a model with the denominators defined and will complete the picture by shading in the correct areas to make equivalent fractions and then labeling the different parts.

UDL Connections

Draw pictures to depict concepts (formative assessment): Students work collaboratively on task. (2.5 Illustrate through multiple media; 8.3 Foster collaboration and community)

Create a Visual Model (summative assessment): Students can express their understanding as a visual model and in writing with scaffolds provided as needed. (5.1 Use multiple media for communication; 5.2 Use multiple tools for construction and composition; 5.3 Build fluencies with graduated support for practice/performance)

Step 4: Methods and Materials

Mrs. Hooks considered her assessments related to her standards-based goals and used her UDL planning sheet (at the end of the chapter) to design methods and materials to support instruction aligned to her LLs' needs and her students' IEPs. Having identified the barriers related to vocabulary, she focused on designing supports to minimize those barriers.

Think Alouds

Addressing barriers related to math: Vocabulary

Mrs. Hooks knows that many students struggle with equivalent fractions because they don't understand the basic concept that a fraction is a part of a whole. LLs in particular often miss this aspect of instruction and try to memorize patterns when adding or doing other operations with fractions, instead of truly understanding. For this reason, she decided to start her lesson by reviewing the vocabulary associated with finding equivalent fractions. **Building the academic knowledge** that is necessary to access the lesson and providing opportunities for practice will **make the input comprehensible** for all students, and especially the newcomers and the LTLLs, so that they can focus on the math concepts.

Mrs. Hooks **established a clear purpose** for the next part of the lesson. She told students that they were going to *create a fraction* as a class. She started by reviewing a core concept as a warm-up, encouraging them to use key vocabulary related to fractions (e.g., *whole, one half, one quarter*). She placed a big picture of a circle on her whiteboard and asked students to tell her what they saw. Students responded by telling here there was a "circle" and a "whole circle". She told them that the number 1 is also a *whole number* and reminded the students that they had been learning about whole numbers. She then separated the circle into two equal pieces and took away one part. She asked the students how much was left, and they replied that half of a circle was there. She wrote the word "half" on the board, affirming to them that they were correct. She asked everyone to stop and draw what they saw on the board, giving the students who were first encountering the words some additional time to process the concepts and language.

She put the second half of the circle on the board again and asked students how they would write *half* numerically. One student eagerly volunteered and confidently wrote ½ on the board. She asked the student to explain how the word half is the same as the number ½. This student, who has a learning disability, enjoys explaining concepts and showing how things work. He demonstrated to the class that there were two parts to the circle and showed how he removed one, leaving 1 of 2 which equals ½. In this way, he practiced using academic language related to math and his peers could hear him thinking aloud and using key vocabulary. This collaborative discussion **fostered interactions in the target language**, allowing students to hear and use mathematical terms used in context by the teacher and by peers.

Four-Square Graphic Organizer

Addressing barriers related to math: Vocabulary

Mrs. Hooks is aware that it helps the LLs to see the written form as well as hear the word when they learn new vocabulary words. As part of her instructional methods, she incorporated two complementary strategies she had learned for teaching vocabulary, the *four-square graphic organizer* and the *six-step process of building academic vocabulary* (see the sidebar "Two Research-Based Strategies for Building Academic Vocabulary"). These strategies allowed her to address the needs of the diverse learners in her classroom, giving students varied ways to represent and practice using vocabulary in context. For the newcomers, these strategies provided structured and **explicit vocabulary instruction**. For the LTLLs, these strategies provided practice using vocabulary in context and allowed them to craft sentences based on their existing language skills. It also helped the LTLLs to connect the spelling of a word to the sound because most of them had heard many of the vocabulary words but did not realize it because they did not recognize the spelling.

She asked students to return to their desks and take out their personal dictionaries to learn the new word, *equivalent*. The personal dictionaries are notebooks separated with alphabetical dividers in which the students write down the vocabulary that they learn in each of their classes. Mrs. Hooks used an adapted four-square graphic organizer (for more information see the sidebar "Two Research-Based Strategies for Building Academic Vocabulary") to teach vocabulary, and students drew the same organizer in their personal dictionaries. Mrs. Hooks adapted the four-square graphic organizer and included a few additional elements to develop students' understanding more deeply. She also gave students the option to use index cards and write the word on the back, so that they can use them to study. She placed the vocabulary word in the middle of the squares in order to project on the screen and model the process (see Figure 5.1). The four sections in her adapted graphic organizer include 1) a definition in students' own words, 2) words in the word family and synonyms to **connect to prior knowledge**, 3) the sentence from the text where the word is used to **contextualize**, and 4) a non-linguistic representation (ex. image, picture, or equation). (For additional examples of four-square graphic organizers, and a related graphic organizer known as the Frayer model, see Dunston & Tyminski, 2013.) She goes through the same process when she teaches new vocabulary in all of her classes, ensuring that students are familiar with the format and can focus on the word.

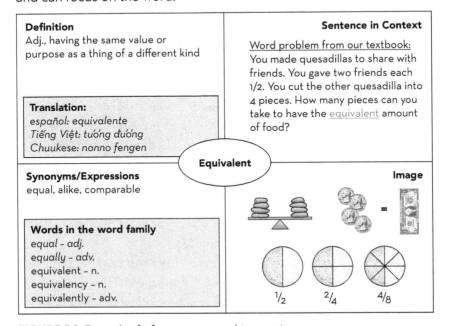

FIGURE 5.1: Example of a four-square graphic organizer

Two Research-Based Strategies for Building Academic Vocabulary

The four-square graphic organizer (Dunston & Tyminski, 2013)

This tool is created by dividing an index card into four squares. Students fill in each of the squares with information to help them develop a deep understanding of the vocabulary word being studied. Each of the four boxes are for 1) the word, 2) a definition, 3) a "lightbulb word" that the student chooses, which serves to remind them of the meaning, and 4) an image, picture, equation, or any other non-linguistic representation of the term.

Six-Step Process for Building Academic Vocabulary

Marzano (2004) has identified this six-step process for building academic vocabulary

1. Describe, explain, and get examples of the new term.
2. Restate explanation and definitions in your own words.
3. Create non-linguistic representations.
4. Do activities that help add to your knowledge of terms.
5. Discuss the vocabulary with one another.
6. Play games that utilize the vocabulary.

Six-Step Process for Building Academic Vocabulary

Addressing barriers related to math: Vocabulary

After students had seen the word used in context, she wanted them to internalize the meaning by **practicing** and restating the definition. To **provide**

scaffolding to support language development, she adapted the six-step process for building academic vocabulary (Marzano, 2004; see the "Two Research-Based Strategies for Building Academic Vocabulary") in this way to align with her use of the four-square graphic organizer:

- For Steps 1 and 2, she asked students to turn to a partner and use their own words to explain the new term to each other.

- For Step 3, she showed a few pictures and had the students draw their own representation of their understanding of the word. She reminded the students that they don't have to be great artists, but as long as they are making a connection with the visual representation, it will help them to remember the new word.

- For Step 4, she encouraged students to write down or use Google Translate on the classroom computer to identify the word in their first language or any other languages that they speak and to add synonyms and other common uses of the word.

- For Step 5, she had each student create their own sentence using the vocabulary word and share them in groups.

- For Step 6, she played games with the vocabulary words to review concepts at the end of the unit.

UDL Connections

Provide multiple options for learning and expressing core vocabulary words related to math concepts, including visual representations and text representations. (Guideline 2; all checkpoints 2.1, 2.2. 2.3, 2.4, 2.5)

Model the use of academic vocabulary and provide opportunities for students to use the vocabulary in sentences. (2.1 Clarify vocabulary and symbols; 2.4) Promote understanding across languages; 2.5 Illustrate through multiple media; 3.1 Activate or supply background knowledge; 3.2 Highlight patterns, critical features, big ideas, and relationships; 3.3 Guide information processing, visualization, and manipulation)

Address of the variability of learners and their language acquisition levels by building in time for students to stop and process information. (7.3 Minimize threats and distractions)

Encourage newer language learners to visually depict concepts in their notebooks, circulate, and give mastery-oriented feedback, encouraging students to add words as appropriate for their level of understanding. (8.4 Mastery-oriented feedback)

Provide opportunities for students to practice using vocabulary in context. (5.3 Build fluencies with graduated support for practice/performance)

Authentic Connections

Addressing barriers related to math: Vocabulary and cultural considerations

Mrs. Hooks knows that students do not always see the relevance in math lessons. To engage students with connections to their own lives and cultural backgrounds, Mrs. Hooks uses strategies that encourage them to engage in the discussion in active and dynamic ways. With these strategies, Mrs. Hooks ensures that all students participate actively and can hear and use the vocabulary regardless of their language learning levels or needs.

To further reinforce what equivalent fractions are and **make the content comprehensible**, Mrs. Hooks instructed her 24 students to stand up and count off. Mrs. Hooks asked 12 of the students to move to one side of the class and the remaining students to move to the other. She asked each group to come up with a statement that describes what *fraction* of the *whole* is on each side and gave them a minute. Each group correctly stated that there were 12 out of 24 students on each side, which equals ½. She then had each half split into two groups and explained that now there were four groups, so the *whole* is 4/4 and two groups is 2/4. She asked the students how many students were in ½ of the class and how many were in 2/4 of the class. The students counted and told her that it was the same. She then told them that they had just described *equivalent* fractions. Students enjoyed practicing the concept this way and it gave a great opportunity for physical movement for her students who struggle to sit still for long periods of time. Throughout this exercise, Mrs. Hooks used **academic language** related to fractions and called on students to state and use the language themselves. She knew that some of the newer language learners might not fully comprehend the more complex terms but that it helped them to hear the terms used in context.

She further reinforced and **contextualized** the concept by making more authentic connections. She told students that they all know a lot about fractions already and that they use them all the time. She started by asking how many students have purchased snacks at the school store (with real money or with earned "star dollars" for positive behavior). She showed them a real dollar from her wallet. She asked the students how many dollars she had, and they answered that she had one. She then asked them if it was a *whole* dollar or part of a dollar, and they all agreed that it was a whole. Then, she took out quarters and asked them how many quarters are in a dollar. They all knew that there are 4, and she wrote the fraction on the board, just like she did when she split the class into fourths. Then, she asked the students if they had one dollar and they bought an ice cream at the store for 50 cents, how much money would they have left. She had pictures of the dollar and quarters on the board and had a pair of students come up and show the class. She then asked what fraction of the money they used and helped the students identify that they had used ½ to correctly represent the amount. She then helped the students make the connection that ½ and 2/4 were equivalent.

To connect the vocabulary of this lesson to authentic experiences and **contextualize** her instruction, Mrs. Hooks engaged students in a discussion about things they regularly divide into fractional parts to share. She asked students to think about foods they share with their siblings, cousins, or friends. To build in sufficient **wait time** for her LLs students to be able to process and think of ideas, she told her students to take one minute to quietly think, and to write their ideas down if they finished thinking before the time was up. When it was time to share, students called out a variety of foods, ranging from tamarind candy to pizza to hot chips. She asked them to think about how they could share half of their food with someone else. One student, who generally liked to make jokes, insisted that he could not share his food because it was impossible to cut tamarind candy in half, and everyone laughed. The student who said she likes chips said she would count out 20 chips and give away 10 to her sibling. Mrs. Hooks knew that this student had some proficiency with the vocabulary, so she asked her to state that as a fraction. When the student said that 10 out of 20 equals one half, Mrs. Hooks asked her to write that on the board. The student wrote the fraction 10/20 and the word *half*. Mrs. Hooks asked her for another way to write half and the student wrote ½. To **reinforce the use of academic language,** Mrs. Hooks encouraged the student to state the terms she had written, and she had the class repeat them.

She asked all the students to think about how that student could share her chips if two more cousins came over and there were four people. She asked everyone to take out a piece of paper and draw or write what this would look like. Some students were able to immediately write out 5/20=1/4. Some drew the chips in four quarters. Mrs. Hooks encouraged students to talk about what they had written or drawn, using the academic vocabulary they knew. She encouraged students who were more fluent with the math vocabulary to come up with terms like one *half* and one *fourth*. For the newcomers, Mrs. Hooks said the words and had them repeat them.

To bring this discussion to a close with a focus on vocabulary, Mrs. Hooks wrote two sentence frames on the board and had students complete them:

10/20 and _____ are equivalent fractions.
5/20 and _____ are equivalent fractions.

She selected students to read their responses out loud and made the connections between the fractions they had written and the terms one *half* and one *quarter*. Mrs. Hooks said that for homework she would like each student to think of something they would eat at home that evening and how they could share it. They could bring a drawing of how they split it up or write an equation and a sentence.

Visual Models

Addressing barriers to math: Language of word problems

Ms. Hooks felt confident that with **modeling and guided practice** her students were ready to move on to solving problems. However, because students regularly struggle with the text-based nature of word problems, she knew that she would have to provide additional support and reminders that the concepts are the same even though they are represented as sentences. She taught her students to read through the problem and identify the numerical information and then draw a visual model to help them understand.

Mrs. Hooks returned to the word problem that she included in their four-square graphic organizers and reminded the students of what equivalent fractions are. She had students open their textbooks to the word problem:

> You made quesadillas to share with friends. You gave 2 friends each 1/2. You cut the other quesadilla into 4 pieces. How many pieces can you take to have the equivalent amount of food?

She encouraged them to draw a picture and write an equation solving the problem. She recognized that *quesadilla* was a culturally specific term that would be very familiar to some LLs, but not to all. She asked if anyone could come describe and draw a quesadilla, and a couple of students eagerly volunteered and explained what it was. The LL with a disability struggled with math concepts as well as language, so to address his language needs and IEP goals, she provided him with a model with the denominators defined and the picture already drawn. This allowed the student to shade in the picture and then fill in the associated numerators. Her standard required the students to also explain their answers in writing, but to help her LL with a disability meet his IEP goal, she included on his organizer blanks where he could label the different parts of the equation (Figure 5.2).

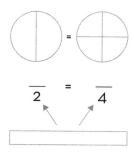

FIGURE 5.2: Visual model with scaffolds

Mini-Lesson: Explain Your Brain

Addressing barriers to math: Explaining and justifying answers

Even though her students could do the math correctly, the textbook and their assessments require the students **to also explain and justify their answers.** This posed an additional challenge for her LLs, so Mrs. Hooks taught a mini-lesson on explaining and justifying answers, including telling them that it meant they had to "explain their brain" by writing a sentence explaining why their answer was correct. She also provided the students with a more robust **sentence frame and vocabulary list** that they could use when writing out justifications for their answers.

_____ and _____ are equivalent _____ because _____.

Mrs. Hooks walked around the classroom giving **just-in-time feedback** as the students were working. For example, one student only drew one quesadilla and divided it in half and then divided one of the halves into four pieces. Mrs. Hooks asked him to look at the problem and see how many quesadillas were described in the problem. She drew his attention to the word *other*, where it said, "You cut the *other* quesadilla" and asked him what clue that gave him, and he lit up and said that meant there were two! He quickly erased his drawing and began drawing two circles to represent the problem. When they were all finished, the students compared their answers in pairs and read their sentence justifying their answers. Mrs. Hooks **intentionally partnered** lower-level LLs with more proficient speakers and her students who were more verbal were paired with some of her students who could help them slow down and pay attention to details in the language. They discussed their answers and sentences when they had differences. She noticed that one of the LL students who often struggled had done the problem correctly. She asked that student to draw his picture and equation on the board and for his partner to read their justification. She noticed the student quietly smiling after he returned to his seat, and she hoped that this small success would help increase his confidence and motivation to continue.

UDL Connections

Provide connections to background knowledge and personal experiences. (3.1 Activate or supply background knowledge; 7.2 Optimize relevance, value, and authenticity)

Provide opportunities to practice and express concepts in varied ways and formats (e.g., moving around and using language and vocabulary to describe what they are doing). (2.4 Promote understanding across languages; 3.2 Highlight patterns, critical features, big ideas, and relationships; 5.3 Build fluencies with graduated support for practice/performance)

Give students the option to use varied formats to express what they are learning as they develop their understanding of concepts. (5.1 Use multiple media for communication; 5.2 Use multiple tools for construction and composition)

> Discuss concepts with students one-to-one to provide practice for
> newcomers or students with lower language proficiency to engage
> and use vocabulary. (8.4 Increase mastery-oriented feedback)

IN SUMMARY:
UDL-BASED LESSON DESIGN

The table below provides an overview of all the instructional planning decisions that Mrs. Hooks made as she designed this lesson with UDL. Teachers can create and use a table like this to organize their ideas and then transfer them to any lesson planning format of their choice.

UDL DESIGN CONSIDERATIONS	IDEAS TO USE IN A LESSON PLAN
Step 1: Consider barriers, pref-erences, and support needs to address	1. Vocabulary 2. Cultural considerations 3. Language of word problems 4. Explaining and justifying answers
Step 2: Goals	Grade-level standards Explain equivalence of fractions in special cases and compare fractions by reasoning about their size. • Recognize and generate simple equivalent fractions, e.g., $1/2 = 2/4$, $4/6 = 2/3$. Explain why the fractions are equivalent, e.g., by using a visual fraction model. Specific and flexible goals aligned with UDL: • Goal 1: Compare equivalent fractions using visual models. • Goal 2: Explain in writing and demonstrate with a visual model why two fractions are equivalent. • Goal aligned to IEP: Student will draw and label a picture to show two equivalent fractions with denominators provided.

UDL DESIGN CONSIDERATIONS	IDEAS TO USE IN A LESSON PLAN
Step 3: Assessments	Goal 1: Draw pictures or manipulate objects to show equivalent fractions (Formative) Goal 2: Draw a model and explain in writing why two fractions are equivalent (Summative)
Step 4: Methods	Think Alouds • Opportunities to hear and use vocabulary in context in various ways • Modeling and reinforcement of definitions Four-square graphic organizer • Structured graphic organizer to build and deepen vocabulary understanding • Multiple representations of information within graphic organizer (e.g., using drawings, visuals) Six-Step Process for Building Academic Vocabulary • Guided conversations with peers to use and practice vocabulary • Multiple representations of words (e.g., drawing) • Finding translations and making first language connections Authentic Connections • Physical representation of fractions through student movement • Connection to everyday and familiar concepts (e.g., using money) • Connection to students' lives and personal preferences (e.g., food) Visual Models • Support for students to decipher the language of word problems Mini-Lesson: Explain your brain • Opportunities to explain answers orally to teacher and peers, with guidance, as needed • Teacher feedback and interaction as students work on problems

UDL DESIGN CONSIDERATIONS	IDEAS TO USE IN A LESSON PLAN
Step 4: Materials	Flexible Materials • Personal vocabulary dictionaries • Provide and model completing a four-square graphic organizer for the vocabulary word, including visuals and LLs' native language • Use realia (food and money) to represent fractions • Sentence frames to support oral and written language production

ADDITIONAL RESOURCES

Alternatives and Extensions

	Making input comprehensible	• Provide manipulatives, like fraction bars or fraction circles, that are divided into different sizes, which can be overlaid to show equivalent fractions to help students practice and understand the concept that fractions are part of a whole. • Include independent practice on an online site that allows students to change fractions and watch a visual representation become divided and shaded appropriately to represent the fraction or equivalent fraction.
	Supporting language production and interaction	• If any students struggle with drawing neatly or if students spend too much time making sure that their drawings are perfect, allow them to use the manipulatives as a visual instead of drawing a diagram to solve the word problem.

	Feedback and practice	• Students can check their own answers by seeing if they could make the same equivalent fractions using the circle manipulatives. • After students develop confidence, remove some or all of the supports in the sentence frames so that they are creating accurate sentences independently. • Play a game to practice and reinforce the concept. Create cards with the different fractions that students have learned and one or two more difficult ones to challenge more advanced learners. Give each student one card and have them walk around and find the person who has a card with an equivalent fraction. They will say to each other, "I have _____, what fraction do you have? Are the fractions equivalent?". Once the students find a partner, they stand side by side around the room. When everyone has found a pair, they will be in a circle. Then, each pair will complete the sentence, "My fraction is _____ and it is equivalent to my partner's fraction _____." The rest of the class will show a thumbs-up or say "Match" if they think the pair is correct and they will show a thumbs-down or say "No match" if they think the pair is incorrect.

Connections to the Research Base

UDL-Culturally Responsive Teaching Connections

Culture and Learning

Center for Research on Education, Diversity, & Excellence (CREDE). (2004). *Observing the five standards in practice: Development and application of the standards performance continuum.* Santa Cruz, CA: University of California.

Center for Research on Education, Diversity, & Excellence (CREDE) Hawai'i Project. (2015). Retrieved April 19, 2014, from *http://manoa.hawaii.edu/coe/crede/*

Cummins, J. (2009). Multilingualism in the English-language classroom: Pedagogical considerations. *TESOL quarterly, 43*(2), 317–321.

Garcia, E. E. (1995). Educating Mexican American students: Past treatments and recent developments in theory, research, policy, and practice. In J. A. Banks & C. A. M. Banks (Eds.), *Handbook of research on multicultural education* (pp. 372–388). New York, NY: Macmillan.

Supporting Language Learners in Math

Abedi, J. (2004). The no child left behind act and English language learners: Assessment and accountability issues. *Educational Researcher, 33*(1), 4–14.

Bransford, J., Brown, A., & Cocking, R. (2000). *How people learn: Brain, mind, experience, and school.* Washington, DC: Commission on Behavioral and Social Sciences and Education, National Research Council.

Brown, C. L. (2005). Equity of literacy-based math performance assessments for English language learners. *Bilingual Research Journal, 29*(2), 337–363.

Coyne, M. (n.d.) *Math the universal language?* Midwest Resource Center.

Dunston, P. J., & Tyminski, A. M. (2013). What's the big deal about vocabulary? *Mathematics Teaching in the Middle School, 19*(1), 38–45.

National Council of Teachers of Mathematics. (2007). *Access and equity in mathematics.* Retrieved from *http://www.nctm.org/ Standards-and-Positions/Position-Statements/Access-and-Equity -in-Mathematics-Education/*

Rosa, M. (2015). A mixed-methods study to understand the perceptions of high school leaders about English language learners (ELLs): The case of mathematics. *Journal Internacional de Estudos em Educação Matemática, 4*(2).

Vocabulary and Building Background

Carlo, M. S., August, D., McLaughlin, B., Snow, C. E., Dressler, C., Lippman, D. N., Lively, T.J., & White, C. E. (2004). Closing the gap: Addressing the vocabulary needs of English-language learners in bilingual and mainstream classrooms. *Reading Research Quarterly, 39*(2), 188–215.

Marzano, R. J., Norford, J. S., Paynter, D. E., Pickering, D. J., & Gaddy, B. B. (2001). *A Handbook for Classroom Instruction That Works.* Alexandria, VA: Association for Supervision and Curriculum Development.

Marzano, R. J. (2004). *Building background knowledge for academic achievement: research on what works in schools.* Alexandria, VA: Association for Supervision and Curriculum Development.

Nagy, W., & Scott, J. (2000). Vocabulary processes. In M. Kamil, P. Mosenthal, P. D. Pearson, & R. Barr (Eds.), *Handbook of Reading Research* (pp. 269–284). Mahwah, NJ: Lawrence Erlbaum.

Nagy, W., & Townsend, D. (2012). Words as tools: Learning academic vocabulary as language acquisition. *Reading Research Quarterly, 47*(1), 91–108.

Vaughn, S., Martinez, L. R., Linan-Thompson, S., Reutebuch, C. K., Carlson, C. D., & Francis, D. J. (2009). Enhancing social studies vocabulary and comprehension for seventh-grade English language learners: Findings from two experimental studies. *Journal of Research on Educational Effectiveness, 2*(4), 297–324.

Developing Integrated Language Skills Across the Curriculum

6

Chapter at a Glance:

Using UDL to address the following barriers and learner preferences and needs:

Accessing Science Texts
- Vocabulary knowledge
- Linguistic complexity of texts

Engagement with Challenging Content and Projects
- Sustained attention and grit
- Multi-component projects

Demonstrating Understanding
- Overcoming challenges with language to demonstrate understanding of core concepts
- Presenting information orally and in writing
- Confidence with public speaking

Learners' preferences and needs
- Relevance and learner interest
- Emotional challenges of immigrants and refugees

›› Classroom Vignette: Science

Ms. Pierce teaches an introductory-level science course at a community college that enrolls a diverse student population. In addition to culturally and linguistically diverse students, there are many students who have widely varied secondary school experiences and language proficiency levels. Ms. Pierce strives to help her students develop their oral and written language skills and to succeed and persist in this first-year college course. She uses UDL to integrate supports during the learning process to ensure that students build confidence in themselves academically as they learn core content.

›› Classroom Profile

- College-level Science course: Botany
- 1 teacher
- 27 students
- Countries of birth:

    19 USA, 2 Democratic Republic of the Congo, 3 Syria, 2 Cuba, 1 China

- Language learner variability:
    - 1 international student newcomer
    - 7 LTLLs with 5+ years in the country
- Other learner variability
    - 5 LTLLs who came to the country as refugees
    - 3 adult learners with jobs and families

THE UDL DESIGN CYCLE: PLANNING A SCIENCE LESSON

At her college, Ms. Pierce has the reputation of being a very support-ive and engaging instructor. Students who are non-native speakers often choose her section of a required science course, having heard that Ms. Pierce provides a lot of support for language and literacy skills. Over the past two years, she noticed that the demographics of her students increasingly includes students who arrived in the United States as refugees when they were teenagers and who have been in the country for four to seven years. Her course is also popular with international students, most of whom had studied English for many years in their home countries, but lacked the ability to speak and lis-ten well in it. In addition to LLs with varied backgrounds, her courses included other groups of diverse students typically found in com-munity college classes (e.g., first-generation college students, adult learners who were returning to school). Ms. Pierce designed hands-on lessons to engage her diverse students and to give them opportunities for experiential learning (see "UDL-Based Lesson Summary" at the end of this chapter).

Step 1: Identify Barriers, Preferences, and Support Needs

Ms. Pierce had worked with LLs for many years, so she was able to predict many of the challenges that they would face in her instruction. However, the refugee students that she had the previous semester presented additional challenges, so she did some research to better understand where the students were coming from and what barriers other teachers were identifying. She wrote all of the barriers down, and then used these as a starting point to think about how to **make her input comprehensible** for the students and **provide them support for language production**. She also anticipated that some of the students might be shy or reluctant to participate, so she also thought about ways to connect to students' cultures and preferences.

Barriers Related to Science Content Acquisition

Accessing Science Texts

- **Vocabulary Knowledge**
- **Linguistic Complexity of Texts**

One major barrier to understanding science is **access to the text**, which is often complex and contains specialized vocabulary that students likely have not encountered in other settings or classes. However, inquiry-based science, like the Next Generation Science Standards, allows for language-rich environments that require students to collaborate and use authentic language to do tasks. If teachers provide appropriate supports for LLs, science classrooms can be ideal environments for language development in connection with content (Quinn, Lee, & Valdés, 2012). As with math, **vocabulary** also poses a challenge for LLs in science. Everyday words that they may be familiar with (often referred to as *tier 1 words*) can have different meanings in science (e.g., *cell, fault, conduct, element*). Science texts also use a large number of general academic words (*tier 2 words*; e.g., *analyze, compare, infer*) and specialized vocabulary words (*tier 3 words*) that are specific to science (e.g., *photosynthesis, mitosis, stamen*) that can be difficult for LLs. Science instruction typically focuses on the tier 3 words because these are new and unfamiliar for most students, including proficient speakers of the language. However, LLs still need instruction in the tier 1 words that have different meanings in science, as well as the tier 2 vocabulary required to understand the texts, directions, and teachers' instruction. In addition, precision is very important in science, so students' use of precise language can be even more critical in science than in other disciplines.

Science concepts and information are regularly depicted through text as well as diagrams, graphs, math formulas, and other forms of representation (Quinn, et al., 2002). While visuals can help LLs understand concepts, for LLs with limited literacy and academic background, graphs, diagrams, and charts can pose an additional challenge if they do not understand how the information is supposed to be understood and interpreted. Additionally, science texts and discourse contain **linguistic complexity** that can be difficult for LLs to understand, such as the use of passive voice to remove the human component and convey a more neutral and factual tone, and the use of nominalized verbs (turning verbs into nouns) and verb phrases to create complex yet efficient sentences (Quinn, et al., 2002). In addition to the language barrier, teachers also report that many of their LLs lack foundational science knowledge, creating a challenge for them to comprehend texts that assume foundational knowledge (Cho & McDonnough, 2009).

Engagement with Challenging Content and Projects

- Sustained attention and grit
- Multi-component projects

Due to the challenging vocabulary and format of college-level texts, LLs can struggle to sustain their focus and attention when reading. LLs inherently require more **persistence** than their fluent peers (Kim, 2011), and **developing grit** in LLs can support them to persist towards their goals. *Grit*, which is persistence over a long period of time to meet long-range goals, is predictive of academic and career success (Duckworth, Peterson, & Matthews, 2007). Developing grit in students is related to having a *growth mindset* (Laursen, 2015), which is defined as the belief that intelligence and abilities can be developed through effort (Dweck, 2006). When students and their teachers have a growth mindset, there are greater opportunities for persistence and academic success (Blackwell, Trzesniewski, & Dweck, 2007). LLs often are treated as having deficits and lacking sufficient language or abilities, and persistence in the face of these attitudes can be even more difficult. However, having a growth mindset has been shown to help students who struggle with negative labels or stereotypes to continue to engage in instruction and succeed in school (Blackwell et al., 2007). To combat these additional challenges, LLs can be taught that growth mindset applies to language ability, which can be developed through their hard work and perseverance (Brooks,

2016). Incorporating activities that honor and give value to students' cultures and background knowledge can engage students and allow them to use their knowledge and strengths for academic tasks. Along with increasing engagement and relevance, this can build a sense of self-efficacy. As students engage in activities in which they can be successful and in which they can see their ability to succeed, they can reinforce a growth mindset that can support persistence in academic tasks.

Grit and the ability to sustain persistence and engagement is particularly important when LLs are faced with **multi-component projects** that they are expected to complete over multiple class periods, and these are frequently included in inquiry-based science classes. Inquiry-based instruction has five main characteristics including questioning, using evidence, evidence-based explanations, scientific knowledge-based explanations, and justification for explanations, and all of these pose significant linguistic challenges and the potential for cultural misunderstandings or discomfort. To support LLs to be successful and develop their language through this inquiry process, students should be given a guide for how to formulate scientific questions and explanations (Cho & McDonnough, 2009). This can be done through modeling, providing sentence frames, including interaction and collaboration with more proficient peers, and text deconstruction.

Demonstrating Understanding

- **Overcoming challenges with language to demonstrate understanding of core concepts**
- **Presenting information orally and in writing**
- **Confidence with public speaking**

Inquiry-based science also requires exploration and questioning and then the **presentation** or communication of those ideas to others, which can pose linguistic challenges for LLs, as well as cause confusion due to varying cultural familiarity and comfort with the process of academic questioning, research, and the sharing of data (Fradd et al., 2001). In addition, presentations and **public speaking** are a source of anxiety for many people, and it is often the biggest source of anxiety for LLs (Aida, 1994). This can be so severe for some students as to "have a debilitating effect on the language learning process" (Wood-row, 2006, p. 309). In addition, language learners often have a lower self-perception of their abilities and, when coupled with the anxiety that many students feel regularly, it can be very difficult for them to perform (Foss & Reitzel, 1988). Of course, LLs also face the added challenge of limited language and understanding of what language forms and vocabulary to use for academic presentations. However, progressing from observation to creating a visual model, and then labeling and using language to describe the model, helps to scaffold the linguistic and cognitive demands in science and helps students to be more specific and to elaborate on their ideas more (Quinn, et al, 2001). Also, listening to others describe their visuals and ideas provides linguistic models that LLs can build upon and provides clear examples of expectations that help students to better understand and feel more confidence in their own presentation of information.

Having to give oral presentations can pose significant hurdles for LLs for academic and affective reasons. Students may understand concepts, but face challenges demonstrating knowledge due to limited language and literacy skills. Students are required to read, write, and speak in order to create and present information, which is a challenge, but the integration of these skills is also the most effective way for them to be developed (Oxford, 2001). Students also need to feel that the activity is relevant and useful to them and need to be supported to focus on the language forms to develop their language (Ortega, 2007) and confidence to present their ideas to others.

Learners' Preferences and Needs

- **Relevance and learner interest**
- **Emotional challenges of immigrants and refugees**

Teachers should also consider individual **preferences** and needs in relation to the subject-area content. Learners are often more engaged if the content is **relevant** to their needs and experiences.

Thus, connecting to students' cultures is an integral part of supporting LLs' meaningful participation in science. Students' cultures and background knowledge, or *funds of knowledge*, are valuable sources of information that can be drawn upon academically (Moll, Amanti, Neff, & González, 2005), further deepening the relevance and subsequent learning for LLs. These funds of knowledge can be tapped into by teachers by making connections to and drawing on students' prior knowledge and cultural and familial traditions as a valuable source of knowledge that supports LLs in developing and adding new knowledge to their existing knowledge.

While the majority of LLs face more difficulty than their fluent peers, due to immigration and acculturation (or lack of acculturation), this is often intensified for refugees, who have been described as semi-voluntary immigrants (Ogbu, 1982) and face additional **emotional challenges**. The resulting trauma from the experiences that refugees can face can inhibit students' ability to learn and succeed academically (Sinclair, 2001). Often refugees will experience PTSD and related symptoms, which in the classroom can look like anxiety, irritability, difficulty focusing, lack of control for behavior and emotions, headaches, and stomachaches, among others (NCTSN, n.d.). Many students also may need to translate for their parents and may need to work or take care of younger family members, causing absences or inability to spend much time on homework. Additionally, many refugee students, although certainly not all, have experienced limited or interrupted schooling due to relocation and war (NCTSN, n.d.), posing more academic challenges than just the language barrier. Furthermore, **discrimination faced in the host culture** can also negatively impact students' self-images, which impacts their ability to be successful. For this reason, in addition to providing linguistic and academic support, teachers need to provide social and affective supports. To start, teachers should put in place regular routines and structure in a calm setting (Gillmore, 2016) and look for opportunities to provide support because students may be uncomfortable asking for help. In addition, teachers can create a classroom climate where cultural connections are valued, and this can engage students and make them feel accepted, putting them at ease and facilitating the learning process.

Step 2: Goals

Because setting clear goals is the first essential step in providing effective **feedback and practice**, Ms. Pierce created explicit goals to drive her instruction and assessment. In addition, she wanted to use a project-based learning approach, which is most suc-cessful when planning begins at the end goal and then the teacher "backward maps" what instruction and supports need to be included to help students reach that goal.

In her beginning 100-level Botany class, the focus is on the anatomy, physiology, and importance of plants. For the section on the importance of plants, Ms. Pierce decided to include a project on how humans use plants for different purposes, specifically medicinal, recreational, and ritual. She wanted to include opportunities for students to bring their own expertise and funds of knowledge to the project and connect it to her botany concepts, so students could choose any plant that meets the requirements for the project, or could choose a culture and pick a plant of significance to that culture. She designed her instruction on the foundation of the Next Generation Science Standards (NGSS), which use an inquiry-based approach. Community colleges often try to align foundational and introductory courses to build on the upper-level high school standards, knowing that many of the students in community college have not fully mastered their high school standards and skills. Therefore, she uses the practices of the NGSS to provide continuity for her high school graduates and to build on the skills and knowledge that high school students are supposed to have mastered. She knows that authentic language use is the best way to support LLs' language development, so she designed her course and projects to support students' language development through authentic inquiry.

Student learning outcome: The students will demonstrate understanding of the economic and social importance of plants (*based on introductory college-level botany course student learning outcomes*).

Related science and engineering practices (of the 8 identified NGSS practices):

2) Developing and using models

6) Constructing explanations (for science)

8) Obtaining, evaluating, and communicating information

The first step in UDL-based design is to consider how to develop specific goals that can be addressed in flexible ways. Ms. Pierce considered how to craft two goals that she had for all her students as they completed a project exploring the economic and social importance of a plant. Studying medicinal plants aligns well with the NGSS and her course student learning outcomes. She had learned that many cultures have traditional uses for plants, including the cultures that her LLs come from, and that if the science content is connected to background knowledge that students already have, learning is more meaningful and fosters engagement (Straus & Chudler, 2016). In addition, she used it as a chance to create a classroom in which her LL students would be able to use their different cultures as an asset and potentially demonstrate their unique knowledge and expertise, hopefully empowering them and celebrating their cultures. To do this, she developed two standards-based goals, taking into account the variability of her LLs and other learners in the class.

Students will be able to:

- **Goal 1:** Create a visual (*model*) and identify the characteristics of a plant that has economic and/or cultural importance.

- **Goal 2:** Create a presentation to describe (*construct explanations of*) and share (*communicate*) research about the chosen plant and its and its economic and/or cultural importance.

Step 3: Assessments

Ms. Pierce planned formative and summative assess- ments to scaffold her instruction and make the learn- ing more manageable and meaningful for her students, while also including opportunities for **feedback and practice** to support language development. Ms.  Pierce thought about how she could design flexible assessments that were aligned with UDL guidelines. She wanted to allow her students to research and present their ideas in an activity that would challenge them to master core content and practice language skills, yet reduce anxiety and stress that accompany complex assignments.

Assessment for Goal 1

To demonstrate their ability to obtain and evaluate information and then to use that information to create and describe a visual model, Ms. Pierce created a workbook to create a **guided approach for students to identify, organize, and plan how they would present information.** The workbook had five sections: 1) guiding questions to help students begin their research and document and organize their findings, 2) a space to draw and label the parts of the plant, 3) a storyboard for the presentation based on information in prior sections, 4) references and sources, and 5) notes to guide their presentations.

To complete the workbook, Ms. Pierce provided additional sup- ports to address the variability of her learners:

- She met individually with students who required more language support and asked them what plant or culture they wanted to research. She then helped them find a short paragraph from two different sources to help them get started with their workbook. She also demonstrated how they could highlight key informa- tion and then fill in the key words, instead of sentences, in their workbooks.

- Students were given the choice to work in pairs or independently. They could work with a partner who wanted to research the same plant and help each other with the research. Students who chose to work in pairs had to complete their own workbooks, but could do so in collaboration with a partner. Students who preferred to work independently could choose to do so.

Assessment for Goal 2

Students developed a short oral presentation (of approximately five minutes) about the plant they had researched, using a visual presentation tool of their choice (e.g., a poster, or presentation software such as Google Slides, Prezi, or similar).

Ms. Pierce provided several supports for students as they developed their presentations. She provided 1) a model of the end result she expected, 2) a checklist of key elements they should address, 3) a rubric of target information, and 4) opportunities for practicing speaking skills.

As with the assessment for Goal 1, students could choose to work in pairs or independently. For those who worked in pairs, Ms. Pierce provided guidelines with clear expectations for each person's input and participation in the presentation.

UDL Connections

Workbook (formative assessment): Provide supports to address variability of learners and their individual preferences and needs. Students collected information on a plant and expressed their knowledge and understanding in a guided workbook which included sections for textual and visual information. (3.3 Guide information processing, visualization, and manipulation; 6.2 Support planning and strategy development; 6.3 Facilitate managing information and resource; 7.1 Optimize individual choice and autonomy)

Short Oral Presentation (Summative assessment): Provide various supports that support oral language and public speaking skills. (5.2 Use multiple tools for construction and composition; 8.3 Foster collaboration and community)

Step 4: Methods and Materials

Ms. Pierce considered what instructional strategies, activities, formats (methods), resources, and tools (materials) that she could integrate into her instruction to reduce the barriers in her goals and assessments. She identified all of the barriers that she anticipated her students, and LLs in particular, would face and designed with those barriers, the need to engage students, and their preferences in mind.

Mini-Lesson: Modeling the Research Process

Addressing barriers related to accessing texts: Vocabulary and linguistic complexity

Addressing barriers related to engagement: Multi-component projects

Knowing that the open-ended nature of a project-based learning experience could be challenging for students, Ms. Pierce started by doing a mini-lesson on the process they would undertake to complete the two assessments for this project **to** **set clear goals and expectations**. Within the mini-lesson, she emphasized vocabulary they would need to look for and use in their own presentations.

Because access to science texts is often a barrier for all students, Ms. Pierce knew she would have to **make input comprehensible** for all of her students, with particular attention to her LLs. For this research project, she provided a variety of sources that her students could choose from to do their research. She selected the sources very carefully for readability and content. She created a simple webpage that she shared with the students that had links to information that they could use for their projects. She included a link to a general overview of medicinal plants to help students gather some background information. Then, she included a list of websites that had information on medicinal plants in the United States and other countries. She made sure to include links to medicinal plants in the

Democratic Republic of Congo, Syria, Cuba, and China, in case her LLs wanted to research a plant from their home culture. She also allowed the students to search for information in their **first language** if they were able to find anything.

To model for students how they could start finding key information on the websites, Ms. Pierce demonstrated the process with a plant of her choice. She included **specific vocabulary instruction**, highlighting words related to medicinal and cultural uses of the plant. She began by discussing the basics of plant-based medicine, and then provided an example of *kalo,* also known as *taro,* a plant with traditional medicinal and culinary uses in Hawaiian culture. She noted that students would fill out a workbook as an assessment and modeled how they could complete sections of the workbook as they found information about kalo from the websites. She also showed them what their end result should look like (See Figure 6.1) when they presented to the class.

Kalo

English name: taro　　*Scientific name: colocasia esculenta*

Medicinal Uses:

- The juice of hā (petiole) stops bleeding.
- The juice of kalo (corm) is a laxative.
- The juice of the lau (leaf) increases circulation.

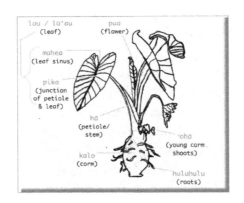

Source: www.healthbenefitstimes.com/taro/; Illustration: Beverly Jennings. Used with permission.

FIGURE 6.1: Model of one presentation slide

She used her model and a picture of the plant to teach the students the vocabulary related to the different parts of plants, which are typically used medicinally. For each vocabulary word, she explained it, gave a definition, and showed images of different plants so that students could clearly understand the word and any variations of the meaning. She provided the students with a diagram of a plant that they could label with the vocabulary words, and spaces to write the definitions for each word, and encouraged them to follow along with her instruction using the handout, noting that they would do the same for their chosen plant in their workbooks.

After she presented the information about the characteristics of the plant that she had chosen to model, she provided more explanation about the cultural significance of the plant and its Hawaiian name,  as well as the English and scientific name. As she did this, she highlighted key phrases and **linguistically complex language** that students would need to use in their explanations. She also provided a handout with key phrases that she was using and that students would encounter during their research.

She reminded students that they could incorporate **personal knowledge and first language** into their projects. She gave them an example of how she had learned about traditional medicines from her grandmother and told the students about her favorite recipe using kalo, and explained that they could incorporate stories such as these into their presentations.

UDL Connections

Provide models and demonstrate the end goals for open-ended or project-based learning approaches. (3.2 Highlight patterns, critical features, big ideas, and relationships; 3.3 Guide information processing, visualization, and manipulation)

Identify resources that are useful and appropriate for varied language proficiency levels. (2.4 Promote understanding across languages; 3.1 Activate or supply background knowledge)

> Provide models of what a presentation that meets expectations might look like to help students understand what is expected; if appropriate, let students know that they can expand on or deviate from the model as they wish. (6.1 Guide appropriate goal-setting)

Relevance and Purpose

Addressing barriers related to engagement with challenging content and projects: Sustained attention and grit

After demonstrating to students what this project should look like, she gave them time to think about what plant they wanted to research and present. She asked students to tell her if they knew of any medicinal plants. Several students related tales from their childhood of plants that their families used as medicines or for cultural purposes.

After this discussion, Ms. Pierce explained that they could **make a choice** about the plants they wanted to present. She wanted to give students the opportunity to use what they know by **incorporating knowledge from their backgrounds and cultures** if they wished. She also wanted LLs to be able to use their home languages and personal stories about their cultures in their research project if they wished. However, she was careful to avoid making assumptions about what students would choose, realizing that students may not automatically want to research plants from their own cultures. Some students who had immigrated as young children or who had left their homelands as refugees preferred to focus on other places where they have lived. To ensure that students had a range of choice, she provided guidance by letting them know they could pick a plant relevant to their own backgrounds and cultures or to the local area where they currently lived.

Knowing that the open-ended nature of finding information, synthesizing key points, and developing a presentation would be challenging for some students, Ms. Pierce provided a clear rationale for the project and the process to help sustain **persistence and grit**. She explained that the students were doing this project-based activity, noting how the process of doing research and presenting their ideas would help them learn essential skills necessary in college courses and in many jobs. She highlighted that the skills they would be practicing were the organization of concepts, presentation skills, and public speaking skills.

She acknowledged that public speaking and presenting in front of others is scary for a lot of people, and explained that this project was an opportunity to practice these skills. Assuring students that they would be graded on effort rather than perfection, Ms. Pierce **reduced anxiety** for the students and made the project less threatening. In this way, Ms. Pierce reinforced **growth mindset** ideals with the students, providing a clear rationale for the research project and for the skills they would learn while completing it. She knew that her LLs, and particularly her LLs who are refugees, would need to persist even more to be successful; therefore, growth mindset and the ability to sustain engagement are even more essential for their success.

UDL Connections

Provide choices that allow students to incorporate personal knowledge and experiences, if they wish. (7.1 Optimize individual choice and autonomy; 7.2 Optimize relevance, value, and authenticity)

Provide a clear rationale for open-ended or complex activities, and an explanation of what students will learn by undertaking various aspects. (8.1 Heighten salience of goals and objectives)

For complex assignments that can create stress, reduce anxiety by explaining how students will be graded (e.g., on effort rather than perfection). (7.3 Minimize threats and distraction)

Foster grit and a growth mindset to support student engagement and persistence through complex, multi-component projects. (9.1 Promote expectations and beliefs that optimize motivation; 9.2 Facilitate personal coping skills and strategies)

Scaffolding Multi-component Projects

Addressing barriers related to sustaining attention and engagement: Multi-component projects

In addition, to sustain engagement through this **multi-component project**, she made sure to provide explicit instructions and a clear overview of the whole project before she began. She modeled for the students how to set short-term **goals** that would allow them to reach the long-term goal of the presentation.

She began by giving the students a checklist with each of the tasks that they would need to complete in order to finish their project. She reminded them that there were two parts: completing the workbook and creating a presentation that they would give orally. She created an **online collaborative progress monitoring document** (using Google Docs or a similar program) where students could enter the dates by which they planned to finish components of the workbook and complete their presentations.

Once they finished a component, they could note their progress on the collaborative document to keep track of how they were progressing and see what remained. Students could set their own incremental deadlines, as long as they could complete the project by the final due date. Ms. Pierce could monitor the document to see how students were doing and offer support to students who were not making adequate progress or had stalled in one step.

For each section of the workbook, Ms. Pierce included **clear objectives, expectations, and guiding questions** for students to use to manage their inquiry. When it was relevant, she also provided

graphic organizers or tables that students could fill in to organize their ideas. For example:

Section 1: Select a plant with medicinal uses that has economic and/or cultural significance.

- Use the provided online resources to choose a plant to research.
  - Optional: Use information from family members to choose a plant.
- Identify the origin and scientific name of the plant.
- Identify the medicinal use of the plant.
- Identify the economic and/or cultural significance of the plant.

Plant name:	
Origin	
Scientific name	
Medicinal use	
Economic/cultural significance	

Section 2: Create and label a visual model of the plant. (*Goal 1, formative assessment*)

- Draw or get a photograph of the plant.
- Label all of the major parts of the plant.
- Complete the table with the medicinal, cultural, and economic information about the plant.

Plant Name:		
Diagram with Labels		
Part of the plant and preparation	Medicinal use	Cultural/economic significance

Section 3: Create a poster or presentation with information about the plant (*Goal 2, formative assessment*)

- Choose to create either a poster or a presentation using Google slides, Prezi, or other presentation software.
- Revise the visual model from Task 2 and include it on the poster or in the presentation.
  - Use color and writing or font that will allow students to see it clearly from a distance (60-point font for titles and 20-point font minimum for other text).
- Create slides or sections of the poster for each of the following areas:

  A poster template and a Google slides presentation template are provided for each section to help students structure and include all required sections and information.

  - Visual model with labels
  - Origin and characteristics of the plant
  - Medicinal uses that specify which parts of the plants and preparations are used for different medicinal purposes
  - Economic/cultural significance

Section 4: Make a list of all references and sources used while developing your ideas and research

- Write down website link and website name
- Write down authors and year of publication

Section 5: Describe the information you will present with a poster or presentation to the class. (*Goal 2, summative assessment*)

- Prepare one sentence to describe the information on each of the slides.

  Sentence starters and sentence frames are provided in this section to help students see the what types of sentences are expected and to provide scaffolding for the language.

Feedback and Practice

Addressing barriers related to sustaining attention and engagement: Multi-component projects

To encourage students to complete the project in a step-by-step manner, Ms. Pierce scheduled class time at each interval when students were assigned to bring a draft of the part that they were working on and they would exchange work and provide **peer** **feedback** to each other. For each peer feedback section, she provided a simple checklist of the components that should be included so that students had a clear guide of what to look for and give feedback on. If anything was missing, students had the opportunity to **revise** without penalty and make sure that they had complete information in the final product. When students finished a section of the workbook, she reviewed each section and provided informal **content and language feedback** in class.

To further support students to be successful with their presentations, after they finished their research and were working on their presentations, she devoted part of one class period for students to practice sharing information they researched in small groups. This allowed students to give each other feedback, and for Ms. Pierce to walk around and so students could ask for clarification if anything was unclear and she could provide students with support for **pronunciation** for difficult scientific terms and for anything her LLs needed help with. All of this support made her students feel much more capable of presenting their information to the class, and this confidence and reduced anxiety enhanced their ability to learn and enjoy learning.

UDL Connections

Provide opportunities for practice. (5.3 Build fluencies with graduated support for practice/performance)

Provide guidance in ways that are non-evaluative and non-threatening. (7.3 Minimize threats and distractions; 9.1 Promote expectations and beliefs that optimize motivation)

Provide mastery-oriented feedback as students practice skills. (8.4 Increase mastery-oriented feedback)

Mini-Lesson: Presentation Skills

Addressing barriers to presenting: Presentation Skills

Learners' perceptions of their speaking ability have a large impact on their level of anxiety and ultimate ability to succeed in oral presentations and other speaking tasks in the classrooms. For that rea- son, Ms. Pierce once again returned to the **growth mindset** beliefs and reminded the students to have confidence in themselves. She decided to include **specific strategy instruction on organizing and creating a presentation and presentation skills** to boost all students' confidence and self-perception of their ability to present information, as well as to support the language and organizational needs of her students. She had them critique a few presentations that she found online. Students identified which elements made a presentation engaging and clear, and which elements they could improve. Together, they generated a checklist with a list of elements of a good presentation. Then, Ms. Pierce gave students an outline to help them organize their presentations. The outline was based on the elements of their presentation slides or poster template with the addition of an introduction and conclusion. She then provided instruction and a list of transitional words and phrases that students could use to connect the different sections of information into a cohesive presentation (Figure 6.2). She also referred back to the example videos with a discussion of **non-verbal expectations for presentations** such as making eye contact, not putting their hands in their pockets, and the use of gestures to engage the audience. She knew that some of her LLs were from cultures that tended to avoid direct eye contact in some situations, so she taught them the strategy of looking at a point on people's foreheads or just slightly above their heads to appear to be making eye contact without the discomfort of actually having to do so. She also gave students tips on how to refer to their visuals and direct their audience's attention to the visuals without turning their backs to everyone. Finally, she again referred back to the video examples to give students ideas about how to pace their presentations so that their classmates could follow along and take notes without losing focus.

She allowed students to do their **presentations in a variety of forms**. In addition to letting students choose a poster or electronic presentation format, she also gave students the option of presenting in front of the class or prerecording their presentation as a video, narrated presentation, or other comparable format. This allowed her to have the same student learning outcome for all students, but reduce anxiety for some by allowing them to record privately and then play the recording for the class, instead of having to stand in front of the class and speak. LLs were able to record multiple takes and revise if they made mistakes, which made the presentation less daunting for some.

Transition words for Presentations
Add cohesion and engage your audience by connecting ideas with transitions!

Introduction
This presentation will investigate/examine/identify/the...
My partner and I will discuss...
Today, I/we will tell you about...

Outline/Preview of the Presentation
Before discussing _____, I would like to describe...
There are # main points I'd like to discuss today, which are: A, B, C and D.
The effects of...will be shown by...

Development (Body)
Introduce a main point
A major _____ is...
A significant _____ is...

Rephrase a main point
That is to say...
The point I am making is...
In other words,...

Introduce a side point
I would like to also mention...
Incidentally,...
Another related idea is...

Conclusion
In conclusion,
Finally, I want to say that...
Thus,...

Summarize/Move to another main point
So, that's idea X, now let's look at Y.
That completes my overview of X, so now I'd like to move on to Y...
Now I'd like to explain...
My next point is...

Introduce an example
This is illustrated by...
An example of this is...

Explain a visual
Now, I'll show you...
As you can see here...
The diagram indicates...

Asking for questions
I'm happy to take any questions.
Would anyone like me to explain further?
Does anyone have any questions?

FIGURE 6.2: Transition words for presentations handout

UDL Connections

Integrate targeted lessons on specific skills (such as presentation skills) that students may not have prior experience with or feel anxiety about doing. (7.3 Minimize threats and distractions; 9.2 Facilitate personal coping skills and strategies)

Provide models of how to present, discussing what is expected and what to avoid. (3.2 Highlight patterns, critical features, big ideas, and relationships; 7.3 Minimize threats and distractions)

Provide alternate formats for presentation (e.g., pre-recording an oral presentation). (4.1 Vary the methods for response and navigation; 5.2 Use multiple tools for construction and composition; 7.3 Minimize threats and distractions)

IN SUMMARY: UDL-BASED LESSON DESIGN

The table below provides an overview of all the instructional planning decisions that Ms. Pierce made as she designed this lesson with UDL. Teachers can create and use a table like this to organize their ideas and then transfer them to any lesson planning format of their choice.

UDL DESIGN CONSIDERATIONS	IDEAS TO USE IN A LESSON PLAN
Step 1: Consider barriers, preferences, and support needs to address	1. Vocabulary knowledge 2. Linguistic complexity of texts 3. Sustained attention and grit 4. Multi-component projects 5. Relevance and learner interest 6. Emotional challenges of immigrants and refugees

UDL DESIGN CONSIDERATIONS	IDEAS TO USE IN A LESSON PLAN
Step 2: Goals	The student learning outcome: • The students will demonstrate understanding of the economic and social importance of plants. • NGSS Science and Engineering Practices (*of the 8 identified practices*): 2) Developing and using models 6) Constructing explanations (for science) 8) Obtaining, evaluating and communicating information. Specific and flexible goals aligned with UDL: Goal 1: Create a visual (*model*) and identify and describe (*construct explanations of*) the characteristics of a plant that has economic and/or social importance to a particular culture. Goal 2: Create a presentation to share (*communicate*) research about the chosen plant and its economic and/or social importance to a particular culture.
Step 3: Assessments	Goal 1: Workbook and labeled diagram of the chosen plant (formative) Goal 2: Presentation using presentation slides or poster (summative)
Step 4: Methods	Mini-Lesson: Modeling the Research Process • Model of what students are expected to do and example(s) of the end goal to demystify steps of the process and expectations • Curated sources of information (e.g., instructor finds websites that have information at comprehensible levels) to provide students guidance with research

UDL DESIGN CONSIDERATIONS	IDEAS TO USE IN A LESSON PLAN
Step 4: Methods continued	Relevance and Purpose • Information provided on how to select a topic • Choices not predetermined for students (e.g., students can make choices that are not related to their cultures/backgrounds, if they wish) • Clear rationale provided for complex projects, and description of how the skills that students are building will be useful in other settings Workbook Activity • Scaffolds for developing ideas and information for complex or open-ended projects • Templates or guidance for students to use • Opportunities for assessment of student progress, and mastery-oriented feedback • Timeline and pace set by students • Collaborative documents (e.g., Google Docs) to share information for students and instructor to track progress Feedback and practice • Opportunities for students to practice speaking skills and to give peer feedback Mini-Lesson: Presentation Skills • Instruction on specific skills that students may need explicit guidance on or feel anxiety doing (e.g., presenting or public speaking)
Step 4: Materials	• Selection of websites with comprehensible information about plants • Templates to guide learning process (e.g., workbook) • Presentation software and posters

ADDITIONAL RESOURCES

Alternatives and Extensions

	Making input comprehensible	• Allow students to research in their first language and ask family members for information. • Provide a few sources at a lower reading level.
	Supporting language production and interaction	• Provide a word bank for LLs to use to fill in their diagrams. • Extension activity: Have students share a recipe that uses the plant.
	Feedback and practice	• Have learners with the same L1 provide additional support to each other in their groups by providing feedback. • Have students practice presenting in small groups prior to presenting to the whole class. Ask them to give each other feedback during the process, using a checklist with specific content and ideas that should be included. Peer feedback without guidance is typically not helpful and can cause anxiety, so giving students something to look for is helpful.

Connections to the Research Base

UDL Culturally Responsive Teaching Connections

Funds of Knowledge

Moll, L., Amanti, C., Neff, D., & González, N. (2005). Funds of knowledge for teaching: Using a qualitative approach to connect homes and classrooms. In González, N., Moll, L., & Amanti, C. (Eds.), *Funds of knowledge: Theorizing practices in households, communities, and classrooms* (71–87). New Jersey, USA: Lawrence Erlbaum Associates, Inc.

Refugee Students

Gillmore, M. (2016). Welcoming refugees in your classroom. *TEACH Magazine.* Retrieved from *http://www.teachmag.com/archives/8880*

National Child Traumatic Stress Network (NCTSN). (n.d.). *Refugees and trauma.* Retrieved from *http://nctsn.org/trauma-types/refugee-trauma*

Pichert, J. W., & Anderson, R. C. (1977). Taking different perspectives on a story. *Journal of Educational Psychology, 69*(4), 309.

Zong, J. & Batalova, J. (2017). Refugees and asylees in the United States. *Migration Information Source, June 7.* Retrieved from *https://www.migrationpolicy.org/article/refugees-and-asylees-united-states*

Language Development Support

Foss, K. A., & Reitzel, A. C. (1988). A relational model for managing second language anxiety. *TESOL quarterly, 22*(3), 437–454.

Ortega, L. (2007). Meaningful L2 practice in foreign language classrooms: A cognitive interactionist SLA perspective. In R. DeKeyser (Ed.), *Practicing in a second language: Perspectives from applied linguistics and cognitive psychology* (pp. 180–207). New York, NY: Cambridge University Press.

Oxford, R. (2001). Integrated skills in the ESL/EFL classroom. *ESL Magazine, 4*(1), 18–20

Science

Cho, S., & McDonnough, J. T. (2009). Meeting the needs of high school science teachers in English language learner instruction. *Journal of Science Teacher Education, 20*(4), 385–402.

Fradd, S. H., Lee, O., Sutman, F. X., & Saxton, M. K. (2001). Promoting science literacy with English language learners through instructional materials development: A case study. *Bilingual Research Journal, 25*, 479–501.

Quinn, H., Lee, O., & Valdés, G. (2012). Language demands and opportunities in relation to Next Generation Science Standards for English language learners: What teachers need to know. *Commissioned Papers on Understanding Language: Language and Literacy Issues in the Common Core State Standards and Next Generation Science Standard.* Stanford, CA: Stanford University, p. 32–43.

Straus, K. M., & Chudler, E. H. (2016). Online teaching resources about medicinal plants and ethnobotany. *CBE Life Sciences Education, 15*(4), 9. Retrieved from *http://doi.org/10.1187/cbe.16-06-0190*

Anxiety

Woodrow, L. (2006). Anxiety and speaking English as a second language. *RELC journal, 37*(3), 308–328.

Conclusion:
Using UDL in *Your*
Classroom

As the four classroom vignettes in this book have illustrated, teachers can develop lessons that integrate various options to support language learners. The variability of language learners, with different needs and from different backgrounds, can pose a challenge. However, with a systematic approach to identifying barriers and considering supports, teachers can build in flexible options, choices, and assessments that give all students different pathways to reach the same goals. We conclude with these three starting points for using UDL to support language learners.

ENHANCE BEST PRACTICES WITH LEARNER VARIABILITY IN MIND

Many of the strategies described in the four vignettes in this book will be familiar to teachers. Some are well-known best practices for language acquisition and literacy for language learners. Using the UDL design cycle, teachers can start by identifying potential barriers and further enhance strategies to take into account varied ways to represent information, flexible ways for students to demonstrate their knowledge, and methods to create engaging learning environments that make it more comfortable for language learners to use the language they are acquiring. Teachers can provide this varied support through the three areas of their instruction that can have the most impact on their LLs, 1) Making Input  Comprehensible, 2) Providing Support for Language Production and Interaction, and 3) Providing Feedback and Opportunities for Practice. With UDL, teachers can consider how to ensure that they design with variability in mind from the outset.

DESIGN FOR ACCESS

The key is to start with the learning goal and to design instruction with a focus on "access" to this goal. One definition of access is "a way or means of entering or approaching." By designing with the needs of language learners in mind, we can ensure that students have entry points to learning and eventual mastery of objectives. By reducing learning barriers and integrating supports that take into consideration the varied needs and backgrounds of language learners, teachers can support students as they develop mastery with language and literacy skills within their content area classes.

The four classroom vignettes in this book highlight how teachers can use the UDL design cycle to identify goals, develop assessments related to the goals, and then use flexible methods and materials to increase access and reduce barriers in alignment with UDL guidelines and effective instruction for language learners. The UDL framework provides a structure and a set of guidelines that can help teachers design with intention and consider incorporating supports in the *continued* areas of student engagement, expression and demonstration of knowledge, and comprehension of information.

Pause and Think

- What type of language learner variability do you have in your classes (e.g., newcomers, long-term language learners, students with interrupted formal education?)
- What are some common challenges (barriers) for your language learners?
- What are some preferences of your learners?
- Think about a lesson you regularly teach:
  - How could you create flexible goals and assessments?
  - How could you apply UDL Methods and Materials to address barriers, preferences, and needs of your language learners?
    - To make input comprehensible?
    - To support language production and interaction?
    - To provide opportunities for feedback (feed-up, feedback, and feed forward) and practice?

As you identify barriers and consider appropriate supports, refer back to the "Chapter at a Glance" sections at the beginning of each chapter to see which specific barriers are addressed and to look for ideas!

START SMALL AND KEEP BUILDING

UDL can be applied in various ways to curriculum and instruction. It can also be used across grade levels and content areas. The vignettes in this book illustrated how teachers addressed language learning and literacy skills in the content areas, highlighting how they selected strategies that provided various scaffolds and supports for language learners. The chapters described ways to use strategies in specific areas (e.g., social studies, mathematics, science); however, these strategies can be used in other contexts and content areas, as well. The key is to consider how a strategy can be modified to address language-learning needs in any context and to actively support language learning within lessons. For example, if the characteristics of some students in one of the vignettes are similar to your students, but you teach a different content area, look at the suggestions for how to address the challenges and the content-specific examples provided and think about ways to adapt or use the strategies or principles in your content area.

As described in Chapter 1, the UDL framework provides a menu of options for teachers to choose from and use as they plan and then implement a lesson. It can be daunting to look at the whole framework and know where to begin. You can **"start small"** by picking just a few of the checkpoints to address and building in flexibility into a lesson. You may want to start by coming up with a more flexible assessment and building in scaffolds to help students succeed on that assessment. Or you may want to consider integrating one or two supports in relation to UDL guidelines along with strategies you already use for an area that your students struggle with.

Once you begin thinking about lesson planning through this UDL lens, you will find that it becomes easier and more effortless to design lessons proactively with UDL in mind. As you reuse lessons over the years, you can add more UDL elements each time, as needed, based on consideration of what worked and what additional supports can help students succeed. Also, consider sharing ideas and strategies with a colleague, because peer support and collaboration is one of the best ways to successfully implement and sustain the use of a new strategy or framework.

A shared goal for teachers is to help students become expert learners who not only learn content and skills but also have a sense of confidence and mastery with their learning. For language learners, this includes giving students a sense of confidence with language and literacy skills that are foundational to their success. Designing supportive lessons for language learners through the UDL design cycle can help both teachers and students feel more confident and successful with the diverse challenges that they both face in their classrooms. Remember, Universal Design is not a one-size-fits-all approach, but a framework for designing flexible supports to meet the varied needs of the increasingly diverse students in classrooms across the globe.

The Universal Design for Learning Guidelines

Provide multiple means of Engagement
Affective Networks
The "WHY" of Learning

Provide multiple means of Representation
Recognition Networks
The "WHAT" of Learning

Provide multiple means of Action & Expression
Strategic Networks
The "HOW" of Learning

Access

Provide options for
Recruiting Interest (7)
- Optimize individual choice and autonomy (7.1)
- Optimize relevance, value, and authenticity (7.2)
- Minimize threats and distractions (7.3)

Provide options for
Perception (1)
- Offer ways of customizing the display of information (1.1)
- Offer alternatives for auditory information (1.2)
- Offer alternatives for visual information (1.3)

Provide options for
Physical Action (4)
- Vary the methods for response and navigation (4.1)
- Optimize access to tools and assistive technologies (4.2)

Build

Provide options for
Sustaining Effort & Persistence (8)
- Heighten salience of goals and objectives (8.1)
- Vary demands and resources to optimize challenge (8.2)
- Foster collaboration and community (8.3)
- Increase mastery-oriented feedback (8.4)

Provide options for
Language & Symbols (2)
- Clarify vocabulary and symbols (2.1)
- Clarify syntax and structure (2.2)
- Support decoding of text, mathematical notation, and symbols (2.3)
- Promote understanding across languages (2.4)
- Illustrate through multiple media (2.5)

Provide options for
Expression & Communication (5)
- Use multiple media for communication (5.1)
- Use multiple tools for construction and composition (5.2)
- Build fluencies with graduated levels of support for practice and performance (5.3)

Internalize

Provide options for
Self Regulation (9)
- Promote expectations and beliefs that optimize motivation (9.1)
- Facilitate personal coping skills and strategies (9.2)
- Develop self-assessment and reflection (9.3)

Provide options for
Comprehension (3)
- Activate or supply background knowledge (3.1)
- Highlight patterns, critical features, big ideas, and relationships (3.2)
- Guide information processing and visualization (3.3)
- Maximize transfer and generalization (3.4)

Provide options for
Executive Functions (6)
- Guide appropriate goal-setting (6.1)
- Support planning and strategy development (6.2)
- Facilitate managing information and resources (6.3)
- Enhance capacity for monitoring progress (6.4)

Goal

Expert learners who are...

Purposeful & Motivated

Resourceful & Knowledgeable

Strategic & Goal-Directed

udlguidelines.cast.org | © CAST, Inc. 2018 | Suggested Citation: CAST (2018). Universal design for learning guidelines version 2.2 [graphic organizer]. Wakefield, MA: Author.

REFERENCES

Brown, A. L., & Palincsar, A. S. (1985). Reciprocal teaching of comprehension strategies: A natural history of one program for enhancing learning. Technical Report No. 334.

Center for Research on Education, Diversity, & Excellence (CREDE). (2004). *Observing the five standards in practice: Development and application of the standards performance continuum*. Santa Cruz, CA: University of California.

Chamot, A.U., O'Malley, J.M. (1994) *The CALLA handbook: Implementing the cognitive academic language learning approach*. White Plains, NY: Addison Wesley Longman.

Crabbe, D. (2003). The quality of language learning opportunities. *TESOL Quarterly, 37*(1), 9–34..

Dobao, A. F. (2012). Collaborative writing tasks in the L2 classroom: Comparing group, pair, and individual work. *Journal of Second Language Writing, 21*(1), 40-58.

Echevarria, J., Vogt, M., & Short, D. (2004). *Making content comprehensible for English learners: The SIOP model*. Boston, MA: Allyn and Bacon.

Fisher, D., & Frey, N. (2009). Feed up, back, forward. *Educational Leadership, 67*(3), 20-25.

Gay, G. (2010). *Culturally responsive teaching: Theory, research, and practice*. New York, NY: Teachers College Press.

Hattie, J., & Timperley, H. (2007). The power of feedback. *Review of Educational Research, 77*(1), 81–112.

Johnson, D. W., & Johnson, R. T. (1999). Making cooperative learning work. *Theory into Practice, 38*(2), 67–73.

Jordan, C. (1995). Creating cultures of schooling: Historical and conceptual background of the KEEP/Rough Rock collaboration. *Bilingual Research Journal, 19*(1), 83–100.

Kluger, A. N., & DeNisi, A. (1996). The effects of feedback interventions on performance: A historical review, a meta-analysis, and a preliminary feedback intervention theory. *Psychological Bulletin, 119*(2), 254–284.

Ladson-Billings, G. (1995). Toward a theory of culturally relevant pedagogy. *American Educational Research Journal, 32*(3), 465–491.

Lightbown, P. M. (2014). *Focus on Content-Based Language Teaching-Oxford Key Concepts for the Language Classroom.* New York, NY: Oxford University Press.

Marzano, R. J. (2004). *Building background knowledge for academic achievement: research on what works in schools.* Alexandria, VA: Association for Supervision and Curriculum Development.

Mathes, P. G., Howard, J. K., Allen, S. H., & Fuchs, D. (1998). Peer-assisted learning strategies for first-grade readers: Responding to the needs of diverse learners. *Reading Research Quarterly, 33*(1), 62–94.

Meyer, A., Rose, D. H., & Gordon, D. T. (2014). *Universal design for learning: Theory and practice.* Wakefield, MA: CAST Professional Publishing.

Noji, F. (2009). *A framework for developing internet-based curricula and course materials.* Paper presented at the Annual TESOL International Convention and English Language Expo. Denver, CO.

Noji, F., Ford, S., & Silva, A. (2009). Purposeful reading. In R. Cohen (Ed.), *Explorations in second language reading* (pp. 7–24). Alexandria, VA: Teachers of English to Speakers of Other Languages.

Pichert, J. W., & Anderson, R. C. (1977). Taking different perspectives on a story. *Journal of Educational Psychology, 69*(4), 309.

Ralabate, P.K. & Lord Nelson, L. (2017). *Culturally responsive design for English learners: The UDL approach.* Wakefield, MA: CAST Professional Publishing.

Rao, K., & Meo, G. J. (2016). Using universal design for learning to design standards-based lessons. *Sage Open, 6*(4), 1–12.

Rose, D. H., & Meyer, A. (2002). *Teaching every student in the digital age: Universal design for learning.* Alexandria, VA: ASCD.

Storch, N., & Wigglesworth, G. (2003). Is there a role for the use of the L1 in an L2 setting? *TESOL Quarterly, 37*(4), 760–769.

Tsui, A.B. (1996) Reticence and anxiety in second language learning. In K.M. Bailey and D. Nunan (eds.) *Voices From the Language Classroom* (pp. 145–167). New York, NY: Cambridge University Press.

Walqui, A. (2006). Scaffolding instruction for English language learners: A conceptual framework. *International Journal of Bilingual Education and Bilingualism, 9*(2), 159–180.

Walqui, A. (2017, March). Quality teaching for English learners. Presented at the annual TESOL International Convention and Language Expo, Seattle, WA.

WIDA. (2014). WIDA [website]. Retrieved from *www.wida.us*

INDEX

content
  density and complexity, 46
  making comprehensible, 87
contextual support, providing, 15, 24, 32, 88–89
Coyne, M., 78, 98
Crabbe, D., 11, 17–18
CREDE (Center for Research on Education, Diversity, & Excellence), 15
  collaboration, 49
  cultural differences in writing, 69
  math-lesson vocabulary, 76, 79, 97
CRT (Culturally Responsive Teaching), 3, 5–6
culture and cognition, 5
Cummins, J., 76, 97
curriculum content, filtering, 5

D

deficit model, 5–6
designing for access, 132–133
digital text, 35–36
disabilities, students with, 46. See also SLD (specific learning disabilities)
discourse, being mindful, 14
discrimination in host culture, 108
Dobao, A. F., 16
Duckworth, Peterson, & Matthews, 105
Dunston & Tyminski, 84–85, 98
Dweck, 105

E

Echevarria, Vogt, & Short, 13
effort, sustaining, 48
effort & persistence, sustaining, 136
EL (English learner), 2
ELL (English language learner), 2
engagement, UDL guideline, 136
Englert & Raphael, 48
Ernst-Slavit & Slavit, 76
ESL (English as a Second Language), 2
essays, "grading" collaboratively, 59
executive functions, providing options, 136
expanding texts, 14
expectations
  clarifying, 53, 113, 118
  reinforcing, 58

expert learners, 136. See also LLs (language learners)
explicit instruction, 32, 47, 62, 83
expression & communication, providing options, 136

F

feedback
  content and language, 121
  just-in-time, 91–92
  mastery-oriented, 18–19, 55
  one-to-one conferences, 57
  and practice, 19, 26–27, 41, 61, 96, 109, 111, 121, 127–128
  providing, 17–19
  reading lessons, 26–28, 41
  science-lesson plan, 109, 111
  writing across curriculum, 60, 63
feed-up, 18
Fisher & Frey, 18
formative assessments
  explained, 8
  reading lessons, 29
  science-lesson plan, 111
Foss & Reitzel, 107, 129
foundational reading, 46
four-square graphic organizer, 83–84
Fradd, Lee, Sutman, & Saxton, 130
Frayer model, 84
funds of knowledge, 108, 129

G

Garcia, E. E., 76–77, 97
Gay, G.
  culture and cognition, 5
  engagement with reading, 25
gender makeup of groups, 16–17
Gillmore, M., 108, 129
goals
  identifying, 8
  math-lesson vocabulary, 79–80
  reading lessons, 26–27, 38
  science-lesson plan, 109–110
  setting, 113
  writing across curriculum, 49–50
Grabe, W., 24–25, 41
Grabe & Zhang, 48, 70
Graham, S., 71

ABOUT THE AUTHORS

CAROLINE TORRES is an assistant professor at Kapiʻolani Community College, teaching Second Language Teaching to preservice and in-service teachers and Writing to non-native speakers of English. She also provides professional development on supporting English learners and culturally and linguistically diverse students to K-12 teachers. She has worked in schools across the Hawaiian islands and in Japan. Her research interests include culturally and linguistically diverse (CLD) students, including ELLs and CLD students with disabilities, Universal Design for Learning, Evidence-Based Practices, grit and growth mindset, and writing instruction, including Self-regulated Strategy Development. She holds a PhD in special education from the University of Hawaii at Manoa.

KAVITA RAO is professor at College of Education, University of Hawaiʻi at Mānoa. Her research focuses on instructional and assistive technology, Universal Design for Learning (UDL), online learning, and technology-related strategies for culturally and linguistically diverse students. Kavita's prior professional experiences include working as a school technology coordinator in Massachusetts and as a specialist for Pacific Resources for Education and Learning (PREL). She has worked with schools and districts in Hawaii, Guam, American Samoa, and the Federated States of Micronesia. Kavita is a member of CAST's UDL Professional Learning cadre and has conducted workshops on UDL implementation and technology integration for schools and districts in the US, the Pacific islands, and Asia. She holds a PhD in special education from the University of Hawaii at Manoa.

CPSIA information can be obtained
at www.ICGtesting.com
Printed in the USA
LVHW011023110121
676044LV00007B/418